LOOKING FOR MITHRA IN MALTA

Interdisciplinary Studies in Ancient Culture and Religion
Editor: Leonard V. Rutgers (Utrecht)

1. Leonard V. Rutgers, ed., *What Athens Has to Do with Jerusalem. Essays on Classical, Jewish, and Early Christian Art and Archaeology in Honor of Gideon Foerster* (Leuven: Peeters, 2002).
2. Karin Zetterholm, *Portrait of a Villain. Laban the Aramean in Rabbinic Literature* (Leuven: Peeters, 2002).
3. Richard Kalmin and Seth Schwartz, eds., *Jewish Culture and Society under the Christian Roman Empire* (Leuven: Peeters, 2002).
4. Jodi Magness, *Debating Qumran. Collected Essays on Its Archaeology* (Leuven: Peeters, 2004).
5. Stephen Spence, *The Parting of the Ways: The Roman Church as a Case Study* (Leuven: Peeters, 2004).
6. Miriam Pucci Ben Zeev, *Diaspora Judaism in Turmoil, 116:117 CE: Ancient Sources and Modern Insights* (Leuven: Peeters, 2005).
7. Mireille Hadas-Lebel, *Jerusalem against Rome* (Leuven: Peeters, 2006).
8. Amos Kloner and Boaz Zissu, *The Necropolis of Jerusalem in the Second Temple Period* (Leuven: Peeters, 2007).
9. Yaron Z. Eliav, Elise A. Friedland, and Sharon Herbert, eds., *The Sculptural Environment of the Roman Near East. Reflections on Culture, Ideology, and Power* (Leuven: Peeters, 2008).

Interdisciplinary Studies in Ancient Culture and Religion 10

LOOKING FOR MITHRA IN MALTA

BY

CLAUDIA SAGONA

PEETERS
Leuven – Walpole, MA
2009

A CIP record for this book is available from the Library of Congress.

ISBN: 978-90-429-2160-3
D. 2009/0602/16

TABLE OF CONTENTS

LIST OF FIGURES

ACKNOWLEDGEMENTS

In various ways and for their help over the years of collecting data in Malta, I am grateful to the following: the former (Dr T. Gouder[†]) and current Directors (Dr A. Pace; Mr N. Cutajar [acting Director]) and staff of the National Museum of Archaeology, Valletta, for their assistance and permission to work the Punic tomb collections of Malta; Fr Victor Camilleri for permission to study and photograph pottery and objects in St Agatha's Museum, Missionary Society of St Paul, Rabat; Mr Patrick Galea for permission to publish the carved stone that appears in Figs 16–18; Professor Maria Pia Rossignani for permission to use the images from the *Missione Archeologica Italiana a Malta* in Figs 30–32; Dr Ken Sheedy, (Director of the Australian Centre for Ancient Numismatic Studies, Macquarie University), Clare Rowan (Australian Centre for Ancient Numismatic Studies, Macquarie University) and Professor Sergei Kovalenko (Pushkin Museum) for their assistance with the coinage of the Pontic region; to my friends and colleagues, Anton Bugeja, Keith Buhagiar and Rebecca Farrugia, to whom I am grateful for introducing me to the archaeological sites of the Maltese Archipelago; Keith Buhagiar also supplied the photograph in Fig. 29.

Claudia Sagona

The University of Melbourne
2008

INTRODUCTION

LOOKING FOR MITHRA IN MALTA

THE NATURE OF THE MITHRAIC CULT AND ITS MYSTERIES

No certain path can be traced for the metamorphosis from the worship of Ahura Mazda that formed in the highlands of eastern Turkey and the Iranian plateau (Fig. 2)[1] to the emergence of the Mysteries of Mithra with its nuances of Greek wisdom. It was a cult that reached the height of its popularity in the second and third century AD in Roman territories after quiet beginnings in the east sometime in the first century BC.[2] Commodus (180–192 AD) embraced this cult and Emperor Marcus Aurelius built a temple to Mithra on Rome's Vatican Hill.[3] Beck makes a compelling argument for the formative years of the Mithraism in the Commagene Kingdom in ancient Anatolia, and from here, it was communicated to Roman regions by well-placed citizens as well as the military rank and file. It is likely that Mithraism travelled along established lines of communication and overlapping fortunes between the Commagene Kingdom and Rome.[4]

Mithra had a largely solar identity; he was lord over the abundance of nature and provider of life-giving waters.[5] Iconography of

[1] Vermaseren 1963, 13–36.

[2] Cumont 1896 and 1899, laid the foundation from which many (often critical) studies followed. See Beck 1998, 115–128, for a good summary of the field of research to that date and an account of the evolution of the Mithra cult. Helgeland 1978, 1497, states that Mithraism entered the Roman Empire in the first century AD; Beck 1998, 121–128, for a discussion of the cult's popularity in the second century reaching a floruit in the third.

[3] Jones and Pennick 1997, 58.

[4] Beck 1998, 121–122, §VI; see Helgeland 1978 who discuss the followers of Mithra among the Roman army; also Daniels 1975, 249–274. I find it harder to accept Clauss' theory that Rome was the place of origin for the Mithra cult, Clauss 1992, 21 *ff*.

[5] Mithra aiming his bow and arrow at rock faces and overhangs in order to release life giving waters from the rock is a common theme in Mithraic iconography; see Fig. 35, third figure in the top left panel.

his cult can reflect strong astrological themes depicting solar and stellar signs. He destroyed evil and the darkness it brings and, as defender of truth, he overcame its enemies. In essence, underlying Mithraism was dualism — the "struggle between day and night,"[6] and between good and evil — themes that its theology explored at various levels. In the original eastern religion, Mithra was seen as a go-between,

> ...the mediator between the god of light and order, Ahura-Mazda, and the god of darkness and chaos, Ahriman.[7]

Contracts and oaths were sworn in Mithra's name.[8] The cult's highly ordered structure, loyalty and dedication to right over wrong, as well as its militant character were aspects that were entirely acceptable to Roman sensibilities, especially as it actively swayed believers to willing contentment with the established order.[9]

Mithraism was considered to have universally excluded women, but in recent times this notion has been challenged.[10] Largely based on Cumont's formative work, the concept that women were barred from Mithraic groups became an accepted trait of the cult. David has demonstrated that in a few regions, women were acknowledged for their active participation and were initiated into the mysteries.[11] Generally, however, it would seem that women were under-represented in this cult, and Gates quite rightly argues that the seeds of its failure lay in the exclusivity of Mithraism and in its small gatherings.[12] Overall, we can be certain that it appealed particularly to soldiers, officials, administrators, slaves, freemen and citizens and within these circles, the cult spread at a familial level.[13] On the whole, Mithraism was not taken up by the ruling or equestrian class.[14]

Their places of worship known in the literature as mithraea were located in natural caves for the use of small rural communities,

[6] Cumont 1956, 4; also Jones and Pennick 1997, 59.

[7] Jones and Pennick 1997, 58.

[8] Boyce and Grenet 1991, 475.

[9] Clauss 1992, 39–41; Vermaseren 1963, 30.

[10] David 2000, 121–141.

[11] David, 2000, 121–141, citing the evidence of the grave of a female initiate with her husband in Oea (Tripoli), a slave women's inscription left in the Castra Pergrina (Rome) and so on.

[12] Gates 1984, 176; Vermaseren 1963, 162–165.

[13] Clauss 1992, 33.

[14] Clauss 1992, 33, 39.

modified to enlarge the space if necessary.[15] Clauss argues that, in essence, caves cut the cost of maintenance (an economic advantageous factor considering the modest social status of many of the followers).[16]

> Mithraea were essentially closed, inward-looking, and somewhat secretive structures.[17]

A cave-like effect could be created by cutting or building structures, but cliff faces and rocky outcrops could be adapted to serve the purpose. Close proximity to nature often near springs, rivers and the sea was desirable in the choice of site for a mithraeum and if these were not available, then water was supplied through channels, ritual basins, or cisterns when springs were distant.[18]

Relatively small numbers of followers is one characteristic of the Mithraic cults. Estimates vary from around a hundred to between twenty and forty individuals per centre.[19] Hence, as more people joined the cult, so new places of worship had to be constructed — many have been documented wherever territories were drawn into the Roman world. Aside from sharing a ritual meal there, initiations into the Mysteries of Mithra were carried out in the mithraea. Here, in the evocative setting of the shadowy cave, initiates would be instructed in the passage of the soul, its descent and re-emergence.

Mithraea in larger urban areas and towns were located in rooms in houses, cellars or subterranean built chambers. These chambers could be decorated in rustic fashion to mimic a cave setting and were accessed by steps, sometimes, specifically seven steps as quantities of seven had special significance in Mithraic belief and hence, mithraea often had quantities of seven woven into their design or decorative features.[20] There were seven stages through which a cult member would pass, seven revered heavenly bodies — Saturn, Sol, Luna,

[15] Beck 1984, 369–370.

[16] Clauss 1992, 44.

[17] Beck 1984, 364.

[18] Beck 1984, 370; Vermaseren 1963, 53–54.

[19] Jones and Pennick 1997, 58, estimate around a hundred followers per cult shrine; Liebeschuetz 2006, 197, suggests *c.* 20–40 in each centre.

[20] An example of a mithraeum at Casa di Diana, Ostia was lined with pumice, see Beck 1984, 370 and references.

Jupiter, Mars, Venus and Mercury — and seven gates through which the soul entered to achieve salvation.[21] The clearest example comes from Ostia, where a floor mosaic depicted a ladder and each space (or gate) created by the rungs was filled with a symbol of the seven cult grades.[22] Generally the main chamber when decorated with iconographic works, were structured to mirror the Mithraic concept of the cosmos.[23]

Mithraea tend to follow a similar plan often with one or more ante-chambers, which could be located between the main cult room and the entrance. In these ancillary rooms, utensils and vessels were stored and food was prepared, as ritual dining played a major part in the cult practice. A unifying element of the main cult rooms of mithraea was the division of a central aisle either side of which were benches or podia.[24] The assembled would partake of the communal meal perhaps mimicking the account of a repast shared by Mithra and Sol, the solar divinity, after the slaughter of a bull.[25] Statues and altars were found at regular intervals in some mithraea and a focal point in the cultic chamber was the tauroctony, the image of Mithra straddling a bull, which he kills with a dagger (*e.g.* Fig. 35, central panel).[26] In essence, the bull slaying scene was heavily embellished with symbols denoting regeneration and the fertility such as ears of wheat that sprouted from the bull's tail.

Much has been written on the simultaneous rise of both Mithraism and Christianity in the old world, two beliefs that had at their core, tenets of salvation beyond death.[27] In many respects their paths were overlapping. There are some obvious shared elements between Christian and Mithraic beliefs and some borrowing of iconography. One example is embodied in the Biblical account of Christ's birth, embellished with the account of the Magi, holy men of the original Iranian religion with Ahura Mazda at its heart, who brought gifts of gold, frankincense and myrrh to the new born.[28] The adoption of

[21] Vermaseren 1963, 138–162.
[22] Vermaseren 1956, vol. 1, §299, 140–141, fig. 83.
[23] Beck 2000, 1967, 147.
[24] Beck 2000, 146.
[25] Beck 2000, 145; Kane 1975, 313–351.
[26] Clauss 1992, 44–46, discusses the mithraeum at Aquincum (Budapest).
[27] Vermaseren 1963, 187; Liebeschuetz 2006, 197; Jones and Pennick 1997, 76.
[28] Vermaseren 1963, 25–26; Matthew 2.

Mithra's birthday, December 25, for Christ's birthday may have recognised long standing beliefs,

> ...in the time of Constantine, the new faith of Christianity was taken to be similar to that of the Unconquered Sun, whose feast day, together with that of Mithras, was also at the winter solstice. Why Bishop Liberius chose the winter solstice as the birth of Christ we do not know, but we can assume that his choice took account of the historical conflation of Christ, Mithras and Sol.[29]

In Malta, a curious blend of burials — Jewish, Christian and other elements simply listed as 'pagan' — occur cheek by jowl in the catacombs. The round or truncated circular, rock-cut tables variously known as *agape, mensa, triclinia* or *stibadia*[30] found in the larger burial complexes have drawn the attention of scholars for decades (the tables can be seen in Fig. 75:B, right of the original chamber; Fig. 78, east of the chamber with benches; Fig. 80:1, left of the original entrance). While their function has remained rather obscure, some form of subterranean assembly place, possibly with rituals surrounding eating has been suggested.[31] There are also fully fledged subterranean and cave churches in Malta. While we cannot say that early Christians borrowed directly from Mithraism for these practices, they would not have been oblivious to Mithraic or other trends around them and this cult seems our strongest influence for the *stibadia* to date.[32]

In the close environment of the small islands of the Maltese Archipelago, the tension between growing numbers of believers in both religious camps must have been palpable. Clauss does point out that Mithraic practices soon took on characteristics peculiar to individual

[29] Jones and Pennick 1997, 76; also Clauss 1992, 66; Vermaseren 1963, 187.

[30] Buhagiar 1984, 19; Buhagiar 2007, 26–27; Bonanno 2005, 265–267.

[31] Buhagiar 1986, 29–34, "The crammed space of the hypogea seems to hint, however, that if a meal was actually partaken of it must have been only something symbolical" (1986, 34); Dalli 2006, 38; Bonanno 2005, 266; Quasten 1940, 256–266, discusses aspects of the *refrigerium* (funeral repast), a pagan practice that survived in the fledgling years of the early church; Kitzinger 1960, 17–42, writes on the nature and significance of the table in early Christian contexts. Bonanno 2005, 266, lists some useful off-shore parallels to *stibadia*.

[32] Bonanno 2005, 266, "These rock-cut, C-shaped tables...had predecessors in pagan funerary ritual way back in the Hellenistic age, and even beyond." Buhagiar 2007, 27–28,

provinces, and in the conservative, somewhat isolated, climate of island culture threads of Mithraic practice could have survived for quite some time.[33] Nonetheless, Mithraism was destined to fail and some point to its exclusivity as one fatal flaw as well as the ever-increasing dominance of Christianity that lead to its extinction after the late fourth century AD.[34] The decline of paganism generally is symbolised by the destruction of Marcus Aurelius' Mithraic temple in 376 AD by the Christian Prefect of Rome.[35] In Malta, traces of Mithra were eventually all, but obliterated.

Mithra In Malta

The Mithraic cult reached many parts of the Roman world and it seems an anomaly that Malta should be immune to this popular, yet private and exclusive cult (Fig. 1).[36] There is every possibility that Mithraic practices filtered into the island sometime after the archipelago came under Roman domination in 218 BC at the start of the Second Punic War. No resistance was given by the nearly 2000 troops that comprised the Carthaginian garrison commanded by Hamilcar (son of Gisco), who were stationed on the island. Malta surrendered quietly to the consul, Tiberius Sempronius Longus. From that point on, Malta was considered part of the Roman Sicilian province.[37]

Few have ventured to suggest that Mithra had a following in Malta,[38] instead the focus has fallen squarely on the gradual Christianisation of the islands.[39] In this regard, Malta has claimed a special role after

[33] Provinical variations in Mithraic practice is discussed in Clauss 1992, 46, *passim*.

[34] Vermaseren 1963, 186–192; Martin 1989, 2–15.

[35] Jones and Pennick 1997, 58.

[36] Vermaseren 1963, 34–36.

[37] Livy Book XXI, 51; Bonanno 2005, 131–132, 138, 143.

[38] Swinton 1768, 262, drew attention to Venuti's interpretation (1735) of a Maltese coin, which depicted an Egyptianising 'Osiris-like' central figure flanked each side by acolytes with offering bowls as Mithra and his attendants. The coin is unlikely to have represented Mithra. For discussion of Phoenician coinage with this cultic scene, see Gouder 1973, 6–7, pl. 1:3. Bres 1816, uses such a coin to decorate his frontis page, see also fig. I and XIV. Bonanno 1992, 30, found no sign of Mithraism in Malta.

[39] Bonanno 1992, 29; Buhagiar 2007.

Christ's death, with the strongly held belief that Paul was shipwrecked there on his way to trial in Rome. There are those who contest this event, arguing that the ship ferrying the disciple collided with the Meleda, or the Cephallenia coastline.[40] Nonetheless, Christianity and Mithraism were permeating the known world at the same time.[41] The latter proved less resilient, ebbing slowly from popularity and, save for scholarly circles that have reconstructed aspects of the cult from ancient texts and archaeological finds, it remains a rather shadowy and enigmatic presence in the pages of history.

Ashby, Buhagiar and Bonanno[42] among others have fleshed out life in Maltese Archipelago during the late Punic and Roman periods. Its two main islands, Malta and Gozo, were home to prosperous and bustling communities that if directly affected by the political and economic fortunes of the Mediterranean at large, appear to have survived them without too much upheaval. Malta's economy was fuelled by its superior ports and harbours through which its domestic products — principally olive oil, fine textiles and perhaps salt — were channelled. While the archaeology of Malta and Gozo is fragile, always threatened by harsh climate and development that encroaches on even the most precious archaeological remains, enough survives of the ancient country villas, bath houses, rural round towers, and urban structures to demonstrate that the islands could match the standard of life in other Roman provinces.[43]

Like much of Malta's archaeological record, the focus of exploration and archaeological research has been, for the large part, on the obvious sites in the landscape. Systematic field survey may reveal

[40] The arguments are summarised in Buhagiar 2007, 1–10; Buhagiar 1997; see also Vella 1980, 61–64; Bonanno 2005, 199–200.

[41] Clauss 1992, 72, "Apart from the cult-meal, the water-miracle offers the clearest parallel with Christianity, spreading through the Empire at the same period as the mysteries of Mithras. The thinking that underlies these features of each cult is naturally rooted in the same traditions."

[42] Concerning Roman Malta for example see: Ashby 1915, Buhagiar 1986; Buhagiar 2007, 11–21; Bonanno 1992; Bonanno 2005. For the preliminary reports of the Archaeological Missions to Malta and excavations of sites that date to the late Punic to Romano-Punic period, see: Garbini, *et al.* 1964; Bozzi, *et al.* 1968; Busuttil, *et al.* 1969; Cagiano de Azevedo, *et al.* 1965; Cagiano de Azevedo, *et al.* 1966; Cagiano de Azevedo, *et al.* 1967; Cagiano de Azevedo, *et al.* 1972; Cagiano de Azevedo, *et al.* 1973.

[43] Bonanno 1977, 73–81; Bonanno 2005, 161–163; Buhagiar 2007, 14–21.

many more archaeological sites hidden on currently inaccessible private lands. In trying to identify places of worship of a private cult such as Mithraism that were small in scale, sometimes isolated in rural regions as well as within urban areas and which had a predilection for subterranean and cave sites is inherently difficult (Fig. 1).

Traces may have been preserved within the burial grounds in Malta. Most of the publications concerning the necropoleis of the post-Phoenician and Punic period in the islands concentrate on the Christianisation of funerary practice. Buhagiar, who has published extensively on Late Roman and Byzantine Malta hints at some earlier, pre-Christian influences at play in the layout of some catacombs.[44] In his major study of the burials places, he draws attention to certain ground plans and features within some chambers that are hard to explain using the established arguments for early Christian practice. Features such as benches that lined walls seem out of kilter with the known layout of Christian burial places.

If we can identify depictions of Mithra and aspects of his cult in the archaeological evidence of the islands as outlined in Part 1, then it does not seem unreasonable that places of worship, the mithraea, also exited in the Maltese Archipelago. In the process of etching in the details of what form Mithraism and its cult sites took in Malta, we should also consider the manner in which the mithraea ceased to function. How these sanctuaries came to a physical end has not always been investigated. An example is that beneath San Clemente (Rome); it was opened in 1869–1870 with little regard to the nature of its ancient seal.[45] Considering the intensity of land use in Malta, the possible chambers that have been identified there appear to have been re-used and remodelled to perform different functions, but a few, especially in the catacomb complexes of Rabat, did have their original entrances blocked.[46] Were these chambers purposefully sealed in antiquity by Christians as an act of extinguishing Mithraism in the islands? Certainly some of the possible mithaea in Malta seem to have been deliberately modified and all were stripped of their iconographic elements.

[44] *E.g.* Buhagiar 1986, Hypogeum 20, 138, "This small hypogeum does not have an agape-table and its Christian origin is doubtful." See also Buhagiar 2007, 26–27.

[45] Nicholson 1995, 358, after Guidobaldi 1978, 249.

[46] For example, in Part 2: Saint Paul-Saint Agatha area, Catacomb 22B (Rabat) or St Agatha's Hypogeum 7 (Rabat).

Part 1 of this study concerns the fictile remains with Mithraic iconography that have occasionally come to light in the archipelago and we can only assume that in the not so distant past building works and other disturbances have uncovered Mithraic cultic sites in which these artefacts were located. Most of these artefacts are from lost contexts in private collections, although four horse and rider figurines were found in the deposits of a few tombs (late Punic in character and in context) in Rabat. Our strongest evidence for a mithraeum lies in the artificial cave site in Gozo at Ras il-Wardija (see Part 2).

As there has been virtually no recognition of Mithraism in Malta, we can only estimate the number of places of worship that might have been on the island, and here we have to also take into consideration how heavily populated the archipelago was in the early centuries AD. Estimating population numbers in antiquity is a very difficult task, let alone trying to determine how many places of worship existed. Malta today, has a largely Christian community that can boast an amazing 360 or so churches and chapels despite its population of only 401,880 (as of 1 July 2007).

Estimates of the numbers of mithraea in the ancient metropolis of Rome vary from nearly 700 up to 2000. On the other hand, based on 33 hectares of excavated area in Ostia and the 15 mithraea that were found therein, an estimate of two mithraea per hectare was mooted.[47] Given that Ostia was a substantial urban centre of some 50,000 to 60,000 people,[48] the closest comparison to it in Malta is Rabat-Mdina, one of the principal settlements on the island from at least the Phoenician-Punic period, but its population would have fallen far short of the Ostia estimate. Rabat is still one of Malta's central towns and is currently 27.29 square kilometres in area. Although it was probably smaller in size in antiquity as defined by the Roman ditch that cut across Rabat (Fig. 70), the late Romano-Punic settlement could well have been a high-density urban centre with storied buildings. Diodorus of Sicily in the first century BC described the appearance of Malta's settlements,

[47] Martin 1989, 3 *f.*, gives the population and mithraea estimates for Rome and Ostia.

[48] Vermaseren 1963, 52.

> …it possesses many harbours which offer exceptional advantage, and its inhabitants are blest in their possessions; for it has artisans skilled in every manner of craft, the most important being those who weave linen, which is remarkably sheer and soft, and the dwellings on the island are worthy of note, being ambitiously constructed with cornices and finishes in stucco with unusual workmanship. This island is a colony planted by the Phoenicians, who, as they extended their trade in the western ocean, found in it a place of safe retreat, since it was well supplied with harbours and lay out in the open sea; and this is the reason why the inhabitants of this island, since they received assistance in many respects through the sea-merchants, shot up quickly in their manner of living and increased in renown.[49]

It should not be forgotten that a 2000 strong Carthaginian garrison was stationed in Malta in the late third century BC and Malta, in subsequent centuries, probably experienced influxes of Roman military and merchant populations. Considering the figures for Ostia, we should not be too surprised at the concentration of possible Mithraic cult centres in Rabat-Mdina (see Part 2); we could expect around a dozen or so cult buildings in that centre alone. In reality, many more mithraea may have yet to be identified in rural regions of the islands. In addition to funerary sites with possible Mithraic architectural traits, there are early church structures, comprising simple stone buildings and natural caves that might have served an earlier, Mithraic purpose. Possible sites have been suggested in Part 2.

[49] Diodorus Siculus, Book V.12.2–3.

PART 1

EVIDENCE FOR THE MITHRAIC CULT IN MALTA

ICONOGRAPHY OF THE MITHRAIC CULT IN MALTA

INITIATES INTO MITHRAISM

The eminent Maltese archaeologist, Sir. T. Zammit, first published a superbly carved stela of what appeared to be two warrior figures either side of a youth (Fig. 3).[1] The plaque was found in Mdina, Malta, and was clearly meant to be fixed to a wall or into a niche or was part of a larger altar; as Zammit noted there was still plaster on the back of the plaque.[2]

At first glance, the image can and has been interpreted as somewhat menacing to the central figure. Zammit, for instance, saw him as a young Asiatic prisoner wearing a Scythian hood and destined for ceremonial execution at the hands of two Greek soldiers.[3] He likened the composition to those decorating Etruscan and Greek pottery of the seventh and sixth century BC. The stela has also been interpreted as the ambush of Dolon, the Trojan youth, by Odysseus and Diomedes, recalling Homeric epic.[4]

I suspect, however, that the first stage of initiation (in a seven stage process) into the mysteries of Mithra is being represented.[5] There is no doubt that the central figure is a youth — short in stature compared to the men who flank him and he is beardless — who can be identified as the initiate in the Mysteries of Mithra. While he looks back to the soldier, he steps toward the bearded male. In this context, the two men are of status within the cult representing different ranks. The bearded male (left) who wears a Herculean-like skin cape with ragged edges slung about his neck and a elaborate helmet with flowing crest is no doubt the 'Pater' figure (Father figure) and on the right is Miles (the Soldier figure) who wears a helmet, furling cape

1 Zammit 1934, 156–157.
2 Zammit 1934, 156; Bonanno 1992, §42, 158, indicated it was from Mdina.
3 Zammit 1934, 156.
4 Bonanno 1992, pl. 42, 158.
5 Beck 2000, 147–149, §II.

and casually holds a spear and shield; both Pater and Miles are Mithraic ranks.[6]

The youth has pulled away from the clasp of the Miles whose hand is still closed, but it is now clearly empty. The youth has his left arm firmly under his tunic; only the edge of his cape is visible curling down his left side. The youth's right hand reaches out to gently grasp the leg of the Pater. To strengthen the sense that the youth is an initiate to the cult, he is dressed fully in Mithraic, typically Persian clothing: the peaked hood and cape, tunic, the loose fitting wrinkled trousers, and feet covered with leather or felt slippers.[7]

The Pater figure has a dagger in hand, but no blood is drawn, instead he grasps the youth's Persian hat (the so-called Phrygian cap)[8] as if to remove it. We recall here the motif of the initiate into Mithraism who is handed a wreath or crown on the blade of a drawn sword, the last time he will wear it, for after the rite, Mithra becomes his crown.[9] Part of the ritual involved pushing the crown off the initiate's head and such a moment would appear to be captured in this stela. In this act was indeed a sense of threat, the sword is after all pointed at the youth, and Vermaseren has suggested that this rite "was a final test of the initiate's courage."[10] The youth would appear to have just passed through this ceremony and so we see the Pater figure with only the drawn sword because he has already given the youth the 'crown of Mithra' (in this case, the peaked cap). The youth's eyes are clearly open and he might now be seen as the newly initiated; in other Mithraic scenes, the untested initiate is blind-folded, not yet ready to witness the mysteries.[11] Noteworthy too is the Miles' stance — he

[6] Vermaseren 1963, 131, 138. Emblems of the soldier in Mithraic iconography include the spear, helmet and kit bag, for example the mosaic depicting ladder of hierarchy at Ostia, Laeuchli 1967, 77, pl. 24.

[7] Cumont 1896, 47–48; *cf.* the Persian clothing on a gold plaque found in the Oxus Treasure, Curtis 1989, 52, fig. 61.

[8] Cumont 1956, 154.

[9] Vermaseren 1963, 145; Vermaseren 1971, 40–41.

[10] Vermaseren 1963, 145; Jones and Pennick 1995, 58, suggest that "a painful and terrifying initiation seems to have been required" of initiates.

[11] Vermaseren 1963, 131, "The novice has his eyes bound; he is still blind and cannot yet see the secrets of the myseteries."; representations of blind-folded initiates before the Pater figure with a drawn sword and a Miles sponsor can be found in Vermaseren 1956, vol. 1, §187, 188, 191 and 193, 108–109, figs 57–60.

seems too passive to be participating in a ruthless slaughter and surely his role in this scene is as the youth's mentor or sponsor, who presents him to the Pater.

The stela has an overall Greek aspect especially in the depiction of the men as naked with Greek helmets, but this is not to be unexpected in Roman artistic expression, which valued Hellenistic iconography.[12] Pater's dagger with rounded pommel and sinuous blade is a type used by the Roman army from the Republican to Augustan period, but it was not widely employed until after the first century BC.[13]

A similar scene was painted on the wall of the mithraeum at Saint Maria Capua Vetere. Here the same combination of Pater and Miles figures are present either side of an initiate who in this case is kneeling with hands tied behind his back. Although this youth is naked and the men are clothed, both men carry or wear similar equipment to the Maltese stela: the Pater figure has crested red helmet, flowing red cape and he brandishes a flaming torch at the young man; Miles has a shield.[14]

Mithra, Caped and on Horseback

Two Melitan tombs that date late in the Romano-Punic sequence (first to second century AD) held horse and rider figurines (Figs 10–12).[15] Both tombs are from a Punic necropolis found in the vicinity of Triq Ferris (Ferris Street) in Rabat, when this residential area was developed in the 1950s.[16] All of the figurines are very similar and yet all

[12] Bononno 1992, 15, argues that Graeco-Hellenistic artistic expression reached Malta largely through Sicily.

[13] Bishop and Coulston 2006, 56–57, fig. 26 and pp. 83–88, fig. 42.

[14] Vermaseren 1971, 28–29, pl. 22.

[15] The four horse and rider figurines are held in the National Museum of Archaeology, Valletta, see Sagona 2002, 288, Rabat, Triq Ferris [584], Tomb 11, in chamber A, 1064, item no. 11, fig. 203:1; Rabat, Triq Ferris [596], Tomb 23, 1074–1075, items 1–3, figs 215:1, 216:1, 217:2, the figurines were found in the shaft of a single chambered tomb with figurines of a cockerel, a pig and a possibly second pig figure. Although a date for any burials in Tomb [584] could not be determined as the contents were not located in the museum, the plan (10e) is certainly late in the sequence (pp. 256–258). Tomb [596] on the other hand held late Romano-Punic wares placed in the Melitan Phase VI (*c.*50 AD and later).

[16] Sagona 2002, 1050, gazetteer entry [572], thirty-two tombs were found in this necropolis.

are made from different moulds. Off-shore comparative material was found in the early excavations at Carthage (Fig. 15).[17] Another example is held in a private collection, which is undoubtedly from a find spot in Malta and although the exact context is lost, it is likely to have come from another tomb.[18]

Iconographically, the type can be compared to other representations of Mithra on horseback, although it is acknowledged that the Maltese examples are trimmed of excess iconographic features. Usually representations of Mithra on horse back show him hunting in full flight with bow and arrow; sometimes with animals running beside or under foot (*e.g.* Fig. 43).

The Rabat figurines all portray a male figure seated on a horse with peaked cap, and flowing cape. The Persian nature of the garb is clear and the attitude rather triumphant. They appear indistinct in their features — only one (Fig. 10) has a pleated tunic falling across his legs and it is likely that all of the figures were made in worn moulds. Depictions of Mithra simply on horseback, however, are known from Anatolia, particularly from northern Turkey (Fig. 2) from Pontic Trabzon (ancient Trebizond) and the lands bordering the Black Sea.[19] Coins from the Pontic region dated from the second to the early third century AD can depict Mithra seated on a horse, in Persian clothing and peaked hood sometimes before an altar with flames rising from it (Fig. 14) or with one or both of the torchbearers with torch raised or lowered in one hand (Fig. 13) standing beside Mithra; see below for a discussion of the torchbearers. Mithra represented only as a horse rider is not common in other sectors of the Roman world, but the iconography was thought to make its earliest appearance on the Pontic coinage.[20] One can only speculate why in Malta and in Carthage this motif appears, perhaps the answer lies in the machinations of the Roman military movements. Immediacy in the transference of these Mithraic notions from the Pontic region to the central Mediterranean is suggested.

[17] *Cf.* Delattre 1898, 9, fig. 15, of a horse and rider.

[18] Sagona, Vella and Bugeja 2006, Attard Tabone Collection, §354, 91, fig. 55:9.

[19] Ustinova 1999, 270–275.

[20] Iles Johnston 1992, 310, for a detailed discussion of the origins of depictions of Mithra on horseback, see her bibliography; Ustinova 1999, 272–275, traces the depictions of solar gods on horseback in the region.

One beautiful example of Mithra in a hunting scene is that painted on the wall of a mithraeum in Dura-Europos in Syria (Fig. 43).[21] In this case, Mithra's decorative Persian clothing is evident, his quiver is strapped to the horse's side and he holds the bow loaded with an arrow. In front, wounded wild animals flee, blood splattering as they run and a snake slithers beside the horse and rider.

From the religious precinct of Tas-Silġ came a naïve, but deeply incised graffito that was found on two fragments of a stone slab (Fig. 44).[22] The excavators likened the engraving to an elaborate scene cut into the lintel of a tomb entrance in the hypogeum at Ħal Resqun (Fig. 46), which was dated to the fourth century AD.[23] The Tas-Silġ example has Mithraic traits. The figure with arms outstretched could represent Mithra perhaps on horseback — note the two lines on the large animal's neck that may represent reigns — and running ahead of them is a small quadruped, probably a dog. The disc with rays emanating at the lower edge in this context can be identified as the sun, thus connecting the figure to this solar deity.[24]

A similar, but rather poorly cut scene was found on a carved stone re-utilised in the wall of a house in Gudja (Santa Maria Street), which no longer survives (Fig. 45).[25] In this carving a person on horseback with arms in a position typical of drawing back a bow and arrow has an attendant perhaps holding a lantern up in their right hand and animals run in front of them. Overall, the scene probably depicts Mithra on horseback, Cautes the torchbearer, a hunting dog and their prey.

An unusual scene on a carved stone from Ħal Millieri church site in Malta might also have more to do with Mithraic iconography, than Christian practices. This stone block depicts a male figure with arms raised up presumably on horseback on the left (Fig. 50) possibly representing Mithra as victor over enemies (in the guise of Sol Invictus).[26] Victims fall around and under the figure and his horse,

[21] Mithra depicted as the hunter in Dura-Europos is dated to 240 AD, see Gates 1984, 166–167; also in Vermaseren 1956, vol. 1, mon. 49, 68, fig. 24.

[22] Cagiano de Azevedo, *et al.* 1967 (for 1966), pl. 26:1, the fragments came from Room 20 in the Tas-Silġ complex.

[23] Cagiano de Azevedo 1967, 50–51.

[24] Bauhagiar 2007, 30, fig. 47:b.

[25] Buhagiar 2001, 17, fig. 5:b.

[26] Buhagiar 1976, 75–76, pl. 10B.

some with chop marks on their head and torso. In any case, it is hard to reconcile the components of this scene with Christian iconography. Three horses painted in fugitive black paint were recorded in a Tac-Caghqi, Rabat, tomb,[27] which might also have a Mithraic connection.

Two small statues of cloaked and hooded figures with feet showing at the hem of the cape are in St Agatha's Museum, Missionary Society of St Paul, Rabat, (Figs 23–24),[28] and although they are now of unknown context, they undoubtedly depict a Mithraic figure, if not Mithra himself (no torches are evident). These might be compared to statues found in Europe, for example, a small statue of Cautopates with hooded cape and torch pointing down that was found in Intercisa, Dunapentele, in a vineyard that is thought to have been a site of a mithraeum given the numerous Mithraic finds there.[29]

The Torch in Mithraic Iconography

As indicated in Vermaseren's comprehensive compilation of Mithraic monuments, many cult scenes are often represented on fictile plaques.[30] One example in Malta, again in St Agatha's Museum (Fig. 19) shows a standard held aloft over a winged figure, who holds a torch above his head with his right arm, a gesture typical of Cautes one of Mithra's torch bearers. The other torch bearer, Cautopates, holds the torch down.[31] Both can be seen, for example, in Figure 35 (central panel), either side of Mithra slaughtering the bull. In the St Agatha's example, the figure hovers over a bull of which only the horns and part of the head survive. Wings, not usually a characteristic of the torch bearers, may indicate that in this case the figure represents Mithra as Sol, the

[27] Buhagiar 2007, 29; Buhagiar 1986, 191–192.

[28] St Agatha's Museum, inv. no. S65 (see Fig. 23) and S 64 (Fig. 24), a damaged similar figure.

[29] Vermaseren 1960, vol. 2, mon. 1823, 244–245, fig. 472, this statue of Cautopates is held in Budapest National Museum, inv. no. 30/1910, 1. Other examples can be found in Vermaseren's 1956 and 1960 volumes.

[30] Vermaseren 1956 and 1960 *passim*; see also Clauss 1992, *passim*. Many plaques are illustrated in these volume.

[31] Clauss 1992, 95–98.

solar deity.[32] The lion-headed Mithraic Kronos (discussed below), however, can be depicted with four wings often embellished with symbols of the seasons — hence his connection to the passage of time.[33] A raven is perched on the right of the standard on the example from St Agatha's Museum, which is a feature in some Mithraic iconography.[34] As to the standard, it appears to represent a flame burning from an elaborate censor or lamp skirted by two, possibly three, petal-like bands. The significance of the flame may be to reinforce the role of Sol, light and the rising sun in this context, as Mithra is often depicted with Sol.[35]

> The two torch-bearers are often interpreted as symbols of light, the one for the Sun rising in the morning, the other for the Sun setting in the evening. In company with Mithras himself, who stands between them, they stand for the three cardinal positions of the Sun, morning, noon-day and evening.[36]

Although indistinct, Mithra appears to hold an object in his left arm bent across his body, given the examples found in other locations, this might be an ear of corn symbolising fecundity and hope.[37]

It is possible that another figurine in the collection of a standing bull might also have served a Mithraic function (Fig. 25). Certainly the nature of the clay from which it is made, heavily gritted and red, suggests a Roman-Punic date for the piece. A large portion of the collection of antiquities came to the Missionary Society of St Paul's and thence to St Agatha's Museum through the founder, Mgr Joseph De Piro.[38] De Piro, in turn, had inherited the collection from his father.

[32] Mithra holding a torch occurs in some representations: Vermaseren 1956, vol. 1, §1756, 231, fig. 454, Mithra emerging from a rock with torch; for a depiction of a solar symbol in this case a sword with rays from the hilt, in a similar position, 80–82, §1137, fig. 297.

[33] Cumont 1956, 105–109, figs 20–23; Vermaseren 1963, 120–122, fig. 50.

[34] See Beck 2006, 192–195, for a discussion of the raven present when Mithra dispatched the bull and at another level signifying the constellation, Corvus. For examples of the raven in Mithraic scenes see, Vermaseren 1956, vol. 1, mon. 37, fig. 14 the raven flies behind Mithra; mon. 40, fig. 15, the raven is perched on Mithra's billowing cloak, and so on; see Vermaseren's indexes for both volumes.

[35] Clauss 1992, 96.

[36] Clauss 1992, 95.

[37] Clauss 1992, 98, fig. 63.

[38] Camilleri 1994, 1, 10–11.

Little is known of the contexts in which the many artefacts in the museum were found. The vast quantities of pottery in the collection can be dated to the Phoenician-Punic period and by virtue of the largely complete nature of the artefacts, we can suggest an origin in the hundreds of tombs of the period that are cut into the bed-rock of Malta.[39] Yet we can only speculate that the small number of Mithraic objects in St Agatha's Museum were found in a mithraeum many decades ago.

Zammit made a very sketchy drawing of a human figure that once decorated a 'gallery' in Saint Catald Street in Rabat (Fig. 33).[40] In this case, the figure holds his right arm up and appears to hold something in his hand. It is tempting to see in this figure a representation of Cautes, the torchbearer. The pose can be compared to painted figures in the mithraeum of St Maria Capua Vetere.[41]

A few other traces of decorative features in the catacomb complexes are also suggestive of Mithraic beliefs. Rock cut figures have been identified in a catacomb at Salina Hypogea (St Paul's Bay), in the end wall of the passage, opposite the entrance and in a position lit by the sun (Fig. 29).[42] What is perceived as a central and dominant figure (some 92 cm high) with others gathered around has attracted Christian interpretations,

> I imagine it to be identified with St. Paul. The torso of a man is clearly to be identified as well as folds of drapery.[43]

Lewis saw the group as Christ flanked by Paul and Peter.[44] Buhagiar further identified a tree branch or twig in the top of the panel on the left side. Given the proximity to the possible mithraeum in this complex of tombs and hypogea (see Part 2), a more likely interpretation is that the carving depicts a figure of Mithra with the torchbearers, Cautes and Cautopates either side, under the branches of a tree. One

[39] See Sagona 2002, for documentation of the tomb finds in Malta.

[40] The sketch was originally made by Zammit 1905–1907, 12–13 (= Fig. 33); reproduced in Buhagiar 1986, 32, fig. 7:b, the painting is now destroyed (1986, 37, 164–165).

[41] Vermaseren 1971, pls 16 and 19.

[42] Musgrave 1979, 98, figure on p. 88, Catacomb B. This equates with Buhagiar 1986, 346–348, Hypogeum 5, see his fig. 112 on p. 347, for a plan of the site.

[43] Musgrave 1979, 98

[44] Lewis 1977, 148.

feature that has not been commented on, but which has survived even in the rather indistinct photograph published by Musgrave, is a small circular feature with rays around it that was carved into the wall to the right of the central figure. This could be a depiction of Sol Invictus or Mithra as Sol or perhaps flames rising from an altar.[45] Looking past the misleading vertical gouges that have been hacked into the wall and focusing on the surviving areas, what might be represented is Mithra on horseback in front of an altar, under the branches of a tree (see Fig. 29, sketch). Such a setting and arrangement of figures can be seen on the Pontic coinage (Fig. 13).

Buhagiar notes, "the 'carving' is either unfinished or so badly mutilated that any guess is as good as another."[46] Perhaps this poor state of preservation is, in itself, rather telling having been subjected to mutilation by subsequent Christian elements. Three pottery fragments said to have been found in the tomb have been dated from the second to fifth centuries AD, but the context and nature of this material is far from clear.[47]

MITHRA, SOL INVICTUS AND ASTROLOGICAL ICONOGRAPHY

Mithra at times is portrayed *as* Sol, the solar deity, and at others *with* Sol. This perplexing duality has been discussed by others such as Beck who writes,

> One of Mithraism's notorious paradoxes is that although Mithras is himself Sol Invictus, the 'Unconquered Sun', he and Sol appear in the banquet scene as separate persons feasting together.[48]

Whether banqueting or involved in other activities, these two deities have been shown interacting on numerous stele in Roman contexts.[49]

[45] Small busts of various deities often adorn the corners and edges of larger Mithraic works. Some examples of Sol with rays around the head are illustrated in Vermaseren 1956, vol. 1, mon. 334, fig. 91, mon. 98, fig. 350, mon. 368, fig. 106, mon 641, figs 179–180 and so on.

[46] Buhagiar 1986, 348.

[47] Lewis 1977, 148.

[48] Beck 2004, 96.

[49] Beck 2004, 96–97, lists other contexts depicting both Mithra and Sol together; Vermaseren 1963, 95–98.

There can be no doubt that a finely carved gem found in Marsa, Malta, cut in yellowish green chrysoprase is embellished on both sides with Mithraic astrological symbolism (Figs 4–5).[50] The stone is imported and it is likely that it was the product of an off-shore workshop. Nonetheless, its maker and probably its owner were well-acquainted with Mithraic beliefs. Astrology permeates the doctrines of Mithraic mysteries[51] and in the centre of the obverse side of the gem are Luna and Sol.[52] Above the shoulders of the former are the points of the crescent moon and the cloth she suspends over her head is the firmament. Beside her is Sol, naked except for his crown, boots and cape (one recalls the naked Pater figure with his helmet and cape in Fig. 3, left side). The whip he carries is one of the Sun's emblems; the whip, halo or crown and torch are the emblems, too, of the sixth grade within the Mithraic hierarchy.[53] Around them are seven stars, the seven revered planets of Saturn, Sol, Luna, Jupiter, Mars, Venus and Mercury. All are enclosed within the circle of the zodiac: clockwise beginning with the crab, Cancer, Leo, Virgo, Libra, Scorpius, Sagittarius, Capricorn, Aquarius, Pisces, Aries, Taurus and Gemini.

In other Mithraic contexts, the bull slaying scenes can be depicted within the circle of the zodiac signs[54] and it is likely that the lion standing over the head of the bull on the reverse side of the gem signifies this event (Fig. 5). Here the lion represents the solar divinity, the Sun and/or Mithra and further linked with the lion-headed Aion who governs time and came to be associated with the cult (see below). The lion is also the fifth of the seven grades in Mithraic belief.[55]

[50] Caruana 1882, 122–123; Buhagiar 2007, fig. 181. Caruana indicates that the stone was given by Grand Master Pinto de Fonceca to Louis XV.

[51] Beck 1998, 119; Clauss 2000, 87–90.

[52] The combinations of Sol and Luna are discussed in Clauss 2000, 152. See Ustinova 1999, 273–274, for a discussion of the significance of these symbols in the Pontic Kingdom — the crescent and star symbols, which were emblems of the Pontic royal line — and the possibility that Mithraic teachings were revered in the first century AD.

[53] Vermaseren 1963, 151–152.

[54] Vermaseren 1956, vol. 1, from Londinium (Britannia), mon. 810, fig. 218; Vermaseren 1960, vol. 2, from Siscia (Pannonia), mon. 1472, fig. 375.

[55] Vermaseren 1963, 146–149.

Parallels to these elements are numerous in Mithraic contexts. Perhaps the most indicative is when similar astrological iconography occurs in the mithrea, such as that on the island of Ponza, off the west coast of Italy, and others in Santa Prisca and London.[56] The latter example depicts a tauroctonous scene with Mithra and the two torch bearers inside the circle of the firmament with the zodiac signs arrayed around the circle.[57]

One further note in this regard are the three circles of varying sizes etched with crosses — or stars — that are located on the left side of the doorway at Tomb 7, Mqabba, Tal-Kandja Hypogeum (Fig. 41); the three positions of the sun. The palm that graces the right jamb has an origin essentially deeper in antiquity than Christianity and together, it could be argued, these motifs of stars and palm have more meaning in Mithraic belief than Christian (for discussion of the palm, see below).

After the Maltese Archipelago was drawn into the Roman world, the islands were partially self-governing at the local level, enough to mint their own coins.[58] Of note is the motif on the reverse of the coinage from Gozo depicting an armed soldier with shield, sword and plumed helmet facing right (Fig. 7–8).[59] In front of him is a rayed orb indicating the figure represents the solar deity. On the obverse is Luna with the crescent moon beneath her (Fig. 6). The date suggested for the coinage is towards the end of the Roman Republic, but no certain chronological path has been determined for them.[60] At the very least, it is clear that in Gozo, both Sol and Luna were revered enough to feature on the coinage and that the Mithraic belief would have been easily and naturally assimilated when it arrived on the island. That Mithraism reached Gozo is clearly evident at Ras il-Wardija. It is one of the most distinctive cult sites in the islands, which served as a mithraeum conforming in its plan and features to other mithraea in the Roman world (see Part 2).

56 Vermaseren and van Essen 1964, *passim*.

57 This London (Walbrook) carved relief is also discussed and illustrated in Clauss 2000, 88–89.

58 Bonanno 2005, 159, 184.

59 Sammut 2001, 18–19, pl. 6:6; also illustrated in Bonanno 2005, 159, 184.

60 Sammut 2001, 18, gives a date of *c.*40 BC; Bonanno 2005, 159, 184, indicates the chronological problems of the coinage.

Mithra Emerging from a Rock

Iconography often depicts Mithra emerging from a rock. Generally this is identified as a rock-birth with connotations of the supernatural, his power over the natural world and purity (a sexless conception and motherless birth), but there are no certain texts referring to such an event. The interpretation of a rock-birth suited those proponents who maintained that in Mithraic cults women played no part.[61] This motif may represent a more general theme of Mithra's control "over the cosmos," [62] perhaps in reference to his role in resurrection and renewal — the embodiment of a spiritual rebirth.[63] Depictions of this event can show a naked, adult Mithra emerging from a rock, often with arms raised and carrying identifying emblems of solar divinity, power and light, such as a dagger or torch (Fig. 49).[64]

Nonetheless, whatever the true significance of this motif, a rather poorly carved statue of a naked figure emerging from stone has survived in Malta. It can be found on display in St Agatha's Museum in Rabat.[65] Its original context is lost, but this humble example made of local stone falls into line with the numerous representations of this Mithraic motif in Europe and elsewhere (Fig. 22).

The general image of a human with arms raised up has been noted in the catacombs of Malta. Although these are linked tenuously to Christian belief, the iconography does sit more comfortably with depictions of Mithra emerging from the rock often surrounded by the abundance of nature; connotations of resurrection are probably intended. In particular, the scene from the Ħal Resqun complex, which portrays a sense of abundance, the fecundity of nature, with animals and fish has three such human figures (Fig. 46).[66] The human figures

[61] David 2000, 137–138.

[62] David 2000, 137, *contra* most commentators on Mithra who see the motif as representing a rock birth: *e.g.* Beck 1984, 356–371; Beck 2006, 219; Clauss 1992, 62.

[63] Brandon 1975, 470–478, discusses the aspect of 'salvation' in regard to later Mithraism.

[64] Clauss 1992, 62–71, figs 21–32.

[65] The figurine of the figure emerging from the stone is published in Camilleri 1994, 21, inventory no. S2.

[66] Cagiano de Azevedo 1967, 50–52, discuss the significance of the Ħal Resqun carvings (= Fig. 46) in relation to a Tas-Silġ graffito (=Fig. 44); Buhagiar 1986, 36, identifies the carvings as a creation scene; they are illustrated and discussed in Dalli 2006, 39.

(from left to right) probably represent Mithra as the sun at dawn, the sun during the day and at sunset; or Mithra (centre) and his two torch bearers who represent the rising (left) and setting sun (right). This would explain why the figure on the right is shown upside down sinking below a mountain (the half circle), just as Cautopates is shown with his torch pointing down (*e.g.* Fig. 13, figure on the left and Fig. 35 middle panel left figure). Another from Kalkara depicts simply a human face with arms held up (Fig. 47) decorating the carved shell lintel of a tomb entrance and from tomb Chamber V at Maghlaq, Qrendi. These are highly schematised figures and overall they may be variations of Mithra emerging from the rock (*cf.* Fig. 49).[67]

The enigmatic, rustic figures carved into the wall of the possible mithraeum cave at Ras il-Wardija, Gozo (Figs 30–32) have never been satisfactorily explained.[68] Each depicts a stylised human torso, one with arms outstretched and one with arms raised up (Figs 31 and 32 respectively). The third may have the right arm raised and the left lowered, but the carving was quite poor and marred by a crack in the wall of the cave (Fig. 30). Based on the Mithraic nature of the Ras il-Wardija and the other evidence for the Mithra cult in Malta, these figures can probably be attributed to his devotees. These carvings can be compared to a symbol painted on a pottery fragment from Dura Europos, Syria (Fig. 34), the site of another mithraeum.[69] An accompanying inscription on the sherd reads possibly, "Mithra the bull [slayer]", but the similarity to the iconography in Ras il-Wardija is evident and by virtue of the inscription and the context of the find in Syria, the connection to Mithra is unequivocal.

Oceanus and Mithra

In composite Mithraic scenes, the water god, Oceanus (or Neptune), can be shown reclining usually in one of the corners. He is typically depicted with flowing curly hair, full beard and unclothed upper body (*e.g.* Fig. 35, lower right hand corner) waving a greeting to Sol's chariot as it ascends to heaven, sometimes with Mithra as his passenger

[67] Buhagiar 1986, 37–38, fig. 9:a–c, the human figures are described as orants; also Buhagiar 2007, 30, fig. 47:c.

[68] See Part 2.

[69] Vermasere 1960, vol. 2, §70B, 14, fig. 243 (= Fig. 34).

(as in Fig. 35, lower panel, centre).[70] One such figure of Oceanus has survived in St Agatha's Museum, which was once part of a larger work (Fig. 36), quite possibly similar to that in Figure 35.[71]

The significance of this association between Oceanus and Mithra is thought to surround the water god's role in creation, hence, in some scenes of Mithra emerging from the rock, Oceanus is represented accompanied by the other creative god, Caelus, who governs the heavens.[72] Thereafter, both can make appearances in a supportive role in depictions of activities carried out by Mithra.

The Cockerel in Mithraic Contexts

Believers in the old faith, the devotees of Ahura Mazda, also revered the cockerel, which repelled evil with its crow; it was the white cockerel that was particularly significant to followers of Mithra.[73] Representations of the fowl occur on various Mithraic monuments often as an element within larger works.[74] From the late Romano-Punic tombs of Malta, came a few figurines of cockerels. Significantly, one example (Fig. 28) was found close to three Mithra on horseback figurines (Figs 9–11) in the shaft of a tomb in Ferris Street, Rabat in 1951.[75] The link to Mithraic belief in this instance is highly likely.[76]

[70] Clauss 2000, 152. The iconography of the solar deity depicted in a chariot can be traced back to the fourth century BC in the Taman Peninsula and Kerch (Bosporan) region, Ustinova 1999, 271.

[71] St Agatha's Museum inv. no. S 5. The nature of the figure was evident to Camilleri 1994, 16, who describes the piece as the personification of a river.

[72] Vermaseren 1963, 78, citing the representations in the second mithraeum at Heddernheim.

[73] Vermaseren 1963, 51.

[74] For the cockerel in Mithraic iconography, see Vermaseren 1956, vol. 1, from Ostia (Italy) mon. 279, 134, mon. 312, 143–144, mon. 318, 145; from Rome, mon. 461, 189. Vermaseren 1960, from Stockstadt (Germania) mon 1210, 95–96; from Poetovio (Pannonia) mon, 1496, 179; from Novae (Moesia) mon. 2268, 356 and so on, see his indexes.

[75] Sagona 2002, 287, Rabat Cemetery, New Street [417], 969, Rabat, New Street [421] §6, 972, fig. 139: 26, 140:2–3; Rabat, Triq Ferris [596], 1074, fig. 215:1, fig. 216:1–2, fig. 217:2, 4. A pig with a rider and a fish were also found with the figures, Sagona 2002, figs 215:2, 217:3. A bird's head, possibly a cockerel is in the Attard Tabone Collection, see Sagona, *et al.* 2006, item 361, 92, fig. 56:7.

[76] Bones of a cockerel with developed spurs have also been found in one Rabat, New Street, tomb: Sagona 2002, [430], 982–985, §14. Fig. 153:1; see also Qrendi [398], 959, §2, 'fowl bones'.

PALM TREES AND FRONDS

Vermaseren draws attention to the significance of palm trees that appear frequently in Mithraic bull-slaying iconography,

> ...two palm-trees which are placed on either side under the ears. The fact that these palmtrees [sic] take up such an important place is to be connected with the ideas of the Mithraists about the hereafter. After death they will receive the palm-branch as conquerors, if they have been true followers of their victorious god and have served him faithfully as his soldiers.[77]

Palm fronds are also represented in scenes depicting the torch-bearers[78] and they can symbolise Sol Invictus.[79] In Greek contexts they can signify Apollo with connotations of sexuality and fertility as well as being an emblem of victory — all aspects shared with Mithra;[80] furthermore there was a clear syncretism between the two solar deities, Mithra and Apollo, in antiquity.[81]

Palm trees do occur among the few motifs that decorate the catacomb walls in Malta (Figs 37–39, 41–42).[82] One particular example depicts a palm tree springing up under an arch, which might be a reference to the canopy of the firmament, just as the cult cave reflected the cosmos (Fig. 39) and even Mithra's billowing cape can be adorned with stars in some Mithraic scenes.[83] Significantly, two characters were written close to the palm tree, of these Buhagiar notes,

[77] Vermaseren 1950, 145–146. For examples of palm fronds in Mithraic iconography, see Vermaseren 1956, vol. 1, 66, §42 (4); 69, §54; 136, §287; 143–144, §312; 152–153, §334; 157, §339; 162, §363; 179, §422; 185, §445; 251, §688; 258–259, §719; 292, §839; 294–295, §848; Vermaseren 1960, vol. 2, 63, §1078; 118, §1292 (1); 125, §1315; 180, §1498; 181, §1504; 190, §1558; 391, §2354; 393, §2361.

[78] Vermaseren 1950, 146, n. 16

[79] Vermaseren 1963, 137.

[80] Miller 1979, 6, 19, 35, *passim*; Artemis can also be represented by the palm [1979, 6].

[81] Clauss 2000, 155–156.

[82] Buhagiar 1986, 37, also Appendix III, 410–422, nos 1, 6, 12, 27, 51, 59, 62, 72, 76, 89, 103, which lists the palm tree or frond iconography in the burial grounds.

[83] The carved palm is in the South-East Hypogeum, Tac-Caghqi Secondary School Hypogea; see Borg and Rocco 1972, 72–74; Buhagiar 1986, 190, fig. 60:B. Vermaseren 1956, vol. 1, mon 310, fig. 84, mon. 321, fig. 88, for stars on his cape; Vermaseren 1960, vol. 2, mon. 1727, fig. 448, mon. 2052, fig. 543, for depictions of stars surround Mithra's head.

> To its right are two characters which Rocco reads as a Q (qof) and M (mem). He thinks they form the verb QM (Hebrew qum "Rise", "Wake up" in which he sees an invocation addressed to the spirit of the dead.[84]

But, notably, Buhagiar does not link the palm to Christian beliefs and even casts doubt over whether the inscription was Christian,

> The culture that inspired this decoration seems to be entirely different to the one responsible for the propitiatory incantation but whether it can be taken as evidence for an emergent Christian ethos is uncertain.[85]

It is quite probable that both palm and inscription were inspired by Mitharic beliefs concerning resurrection.

It is noteworthy that in the majority of these representations of palm trees or fronds, they often stand alone without additional, unequivocal and contemporary Christian iconography, such as crosses. The so-called chapel site at Abbatija tad-Dejr (Rabat), which it is argued was originally a mithraeum (Part 2),[86] also had a palm frond incised into the wall. Ultimately, we cannot be certain that the palm signified Christian beliefs. Hence, it is possible that into the mix of Christian and Jewish burials in these Maltese catacomb complexes, were added the remains of followers of Mithra.[87]

ICONOGRAPHIC CONNECTIONS BETWEEN MITHRA AND OTHER CULTS

Mithraic contexts can also depict figures with a lion's head, crown or rays and a human body caught in the coils of a large snake, which overall represented the lion-headed (leontocephalous), Mithraic Kronos or Aion as some refer to him,[88] or perhaps even Ahriman "the great Evil One of the Zoroastrian pantheon"[89] who, in the west, would

[84] Buhagiar 1986, 190, after Borg and Rocco 1972.

[85] Buhagiar 1986, 190; see also Buhagiar 2007, 31.

[86] See Part 2.

[87] Buhagiar 1986, 29, remarks on the mixed nature of the religious iconography in the catacombs.

[88] Clauss 2000, 165; Vermaseren 1963, 116–120; Levi 1944, 275–276.

[89] Jackson 1985, 18.

appear to have undergone a metamorphosis away from his original, malevolent nature in the old eastern religion. Of this representation, one example survives in Malta in a private collection (Fig. 18), which was found in Rabat around the early 1950s.[90] This large stela made of local stone is carved with a lion's head facing the front. Although damaged, enough remains to identify the lion's features. Its ears are rounded and set high on the side of the head and part of the wide, flat feline nose survives. A broad band encircles the face representing the mane and a crown is clearly depicted on the head, but the top is broken away. Traces of lines radiating from a central point and one cross, perhaps representing a star, survive in the upper right corner (Fig. 16). This stela can be likened to statues found in the Levant, Egypt, Italy and so on.[91]

In general, the lion-headed figure is thought to have solar connotations, especially in regards to the passage of time, to the four seasons (see 'The Torch in Mithraic Iconography', above)[92] and the representation of fire.[93] One side edge of this stela appears to be dressed and smoothed and the complete work was probably only a centimetre or two wider than the surviving 53 cm. If it was in fact a representation of Mithraic Kronos, then we could expect that the complete stela appeared somewhat like Figure 17, with a naked human body bound in the coils of a snake.

One other unusual carved stela of uncertain provenance in Malta depicts a thin serpent and a wide cobra either side of a flower on top of a tall stem emerging from a bulbous, egg-like base (Fig. 20).[94]

[90] I am very grateful to Patrick Galea for his permission to publish this stela and for providing its dimensions: 53 cm wide, 40 cm high and 15 cm thick.

[91] Examples of lion-headed, human-bodied statues in Vermaseren 1956, vol. I, from Sidon §78, 73, fig. 29a–b; in Memphis (Egypt) §94, 82, fig. 35; from Oxyrhynchus (Egypt), §103, 83, fig. 36; from Rusicade (Numidia) §125, 91, fig. 40; from Ostia (Italy) §312, 143–144, fig. 85; §314, 144, fig. 86; Castel Gandolfo (Italy) §326, 147–148, figs 89–90; Rome §543, 212–213, fig. 152; §545, 213, fig. 153, *etc.*

[92] Jackson 1985, 17–45, explores all of the various interpretations of the lion-headed figure, ultimately recognising it to have "strong solar associations" (1985, 33–34). The figures are also linked to Aion, *e.g.* Vermaseren 1956, vol. I, §78, §312, §314; Vermaseren 1963, 120–122.

[93] Clauss 2000, 164.

[94] For Mithra emerging from egg-shaped bases, see Beck 2006, 219, who refers to a monument at the Housesteads mithraeum (on Hadrian's Wall).

Bonanno makes a convincing argument that the artefact came from Tas-Silġ and was part of a larger work, possible additional fragments of which were recovered from the site during archaeological excavations.[95] He identifies the cobra as the Egyptian uraeus and the central flower base as an Egyptian *atef*-crown. The missing heads of the snakes possibly once depicted the human forms of Serapis on the thinner snake on the left and Isis on the cobra. A striking parallel is drawn to a stela in Rijksmuseum Van Oudheden (Fig. 21), which is more complete than the example from Malta.[96] As consorts, these divinities symbolise fertility and, like Mithraism and Christianity, in time their cult was widely spread throughout the Roman Empire. Serapis' strong association with serpents has also been linked to traditions surrounding Mithraic Kronos or Aion.[97]

Mithraism was sometimes associated with the mystery cult of Isis and Serapis in other regions of the Roman world[98] and it may be that in Malta, some Mithraic centres embraced Serapis and Isis, incorporating elements into their religious practice. As Vermaseren notes,

> The god Sarapis was sometimes equated with Saturn, but his presence in the Mithras cult proves that this Egyptian deity, often mentioned in the same breath with Isis, was adopted by worshippers of Mithras during the period when the cult was making an all-out attempt at supremacy.[99]

At the very least, the presence of this iconography in the temple precinct at Tas-Silġ, where Astarte was once worshipped during the floruit of the Phoenician-Punic period, demonstrates that Malta despite not lying at the pulse of Roman culture was certainly exposed to new influences infiltrating the Roman world. We might also question the role of this famous temple site and point to a more complex range of worship there in the late Romano-Punic and Roman periods.

95 Bonanno 1996, 46.

96 International inventory number 06/001/14396, inventory number F 1960/9.1, purchased in 1960, unknown provenance. Illustration at: http://www.globalegyptianmuseum.org/large.aspx?img=images/RMO/017930.jpg. Note that Bonanno identifies the work as originating in El Bahnasa, Egypt, see Bonanno 1996, 45.

97 Levi 1944, 276.

98 Liebeschuetz 2006, 196, Isis, Sarapis and Mithra are found together in the Aventine mithraeum (2006, 43–52); in the Walbrook mithraeum, London (2006, 52–55).

99 Vermaseren 1963, 49.

PART 2

MITHRAIC ARCHITECTURAL REMNANTS IN THE ARCHAEOLOGICAL AND EARLY CHRISTIAN CONTEXTS OF MALTA

POSSIBLE MITHRAIC STRUCTURES IN THE MALTESE ARCHIPELAGO

Based on the hundreds of mithraea that have been found in Europe — wherever the Romans made their mark — certain architectural features suggest Mithraic practice (Figs 51–52). These places of worship tend to be small size, with benches lining the walls. The benches served as seating for the followers because ritual dining was one hallmark of the cult. The general ground plans varied according to the setting in a natural cave or beneath urban areas, but generally an entrance lead into the main chamber or cult room; the overall aspect of the chamber was to keep or create the sense of a natural cave. In a number of cases, antechambers were located adjacent to the inner chamber and these functioned as storerooms for cult paraphernalia, pottery and dining utensils. Apses in the rear wall of the main chamber were often adorned with a tauroctony, a depiction of Mithra straddling a bull and plunging a dagger into the animal's side; around this central scene other iconographic details often with underlying astrological associations were added. Niches for cult images, plaques and free-standing altars can be located along the sides of and entrances to the room. In rural areas, mithraea were often located near water source and springs or were supplied with water storage vessels.

Until now, no claims of Mithraic connections have been made for the Maltese catacombs and it has to be pointed out that many burial complexes do *not* have features that can be linked to the cult. Instead these complexes can have simple antechambers perhaps embellished with tomb cubicles or wall niches and doorways that can lead into elaborate catacombs or into rooms and rock-cut tables known by numerous names, but commonly in Malta as *agape, stibadium* or *triclinium* tables.[1] Other complexes open onto galleries of tombs or corridors flanked by tomb niches of various kinds. These catacombs were originally conceived and cut as burial grounds. Certain criteria are used to determine whether these catacombs in Malta were Christian. Principally, the presence of Christian iconography such as crosses,

[1] These are discussed in detail in Buhagiar's 1986 volume.

olive branches and doves and a few inscriptions as well as the presence of the *stibadia* are telling factors;[2] palm trees and fronds are more problematic as they are Mithraic iconographic devices. Similarly, Jewish affiliations can be represented by seven-armed candelabra, as well as by some inscriptions. Other burial grounds fall into an ambiguous category loosely identified as 'pagan' or non-Christian.[3]

There is another range of features in the catacombs, which do not sit well with accepted early Christian burial practice. In 1898, Caruana described catacombs with seating arrangements as,

> ...having all the features of a *Collegium funeraticium* or burial-club of another corporation...rock benches running all round, seemingly fitted for occasional assemblings [sic] of the members of the corporation.[4]

Clearly, the non-Christian features of these chambers and the overall appearance did not fit the range apparent in the early Christian burial grounds in the Maltese islands. To reiterate, the accumulated evidence of Mithraic cult centres elsewhere in the Roman world suggests that there are some attributes of the buildings that are indicative of their places of worship. Benches that edged the walls of large subterranean chambers and well-cut niches often with an arched top located in the rear wall of the cult chambers, opposite to the original entrance, are likely to have once formed a cultic niche when the room served as a mithraeum.[5] In Malta, in most cases, such niches have been cut through at a later date to form a doorway into catacombs and can stand in contrast to subsequent, plain rectangular doorways cut to gain access to additional catacomb galleries. In other words, in some of these chambers that now appear to have served as antechambers to galleries of tombs, one niche will be elaborately finished and is often arched, while additional (and presumably later) doorways are simpler and usually less well finished. In reality, the catacombs reflect chronological development and expansion; they may have ultimately served a funerary function, but some would appear to have begun as Mithraic cult centres.

[2] Buhagiar 1986, 29, 138.

[3] Buhagiar 2007, 25–26.

[4] Caruana 1898, 91.

[5] For example, see 'The Primary School Hypogeum'; Binġemma Hypogeum 26 (Mġarr).

Ras il-Wardija on the west coast of Gozo (the north island) is arguably the most convincing of Mithraic sites in the archipelago (Figs 53–55) with well-cut wide benches, an inner sanctum with large wall niches, nearby water storage facilities and possible Mithraic graffiti scratched into the walls (see Part 1). Considering the Mithraic cult trait to have limited gatherings of followers and thus numerous, small places of worship, we can be relatively confident that Ras il-Wardija was not alone. Caves, troglodyte dwellings and vaulted chambers exist in Malta that lie abandoned, still serve as farm sheds or once functioned as subterranean Christian churches in the past.[6] Some of these sites may warrant further investigation because they may have replaced previous Mithraic centres when the cult ebbed into extinction. These cave churches can be rather isolated such as San Niklaw (Figs 65 and 66).[7] In urban areas, complexes such as the underground church at St Agatha's now enlarged and embellished with Christian frescoes may have originally served the Mithraic cult.[8]

> Christianity and Mithraism had much in common most obviously the ground plan of their respective meeting places.[9]

Unfortunately, in Malta most have provided little accurate evidence for dating.[10] Although not a hard and fast characteristic, there is a tendency for entrance and chamber of mithraea to lie on a roughly east-west axis.

Buhagiar mentions the practice of adjoining churches in some districts (Fig. 69).[11] He suggests that they were chapels built for specific saints, but the presence of benches in some, does throw a mantel of

[6] Dalli 2006, 290–293. Buhagiar 2007, 96, does acknowledge that the "Christian fascination with caves" may have been influenced by Zoroastrian practices and tenets surrounding the rock birth of Mithra.

[7] Cave sites of various known uses in Malta: for San Niklaw, Buhagiar (K.) 1997, 131–137; Buhagiar 1983, 18.

[8] St Agatha's catacombs and church complex in Buhagiar 1986, 94–146; Buhagiar 2007, 98.

[9] Liebeschuetz 2006, 196.

[10] Buhagiar 1975, 164 and n. 13.

[11] Buhagiar 1975, 164, fig. 6, "there were adjoining churches of Santa Maria and Santa Caterina at Tal-Baqqari near Żurrieq." (= Fig. 69), another at Ħal Millieri although only one chapel still stands and the outline of a second is still evident in the boundary wall-line of the compound, see Buhagiar 1976, 74, fig. 5; Buhagiar 2007, 107–108.

Mithraic architectural features over the structures. Although it is argued that such benches may have been a common feature of early churches on the island,[12] there may have been some sharing of architectural traits and practice. Nonetheless, early church structures and natural caves have been listed below that might have first functioned as religious precincts for Mithraic cult followers.

RURAL SETTING

Ras il-Wardija (Gozo, the north island)

No unequivocal mithraeum has been identified in Malta, but Ras il-Wardija on the western coast of Gozo does lend itself to this interpretation (Figs 53–56). In essence, the complex at this site comprises an artificial 'Cave' cut into the rock face on an east-west axis (Fig. 55) and the area in front may have formed a second 'Long Chamber' constructed following a north-south axis (Figs 55–56).[13]

A date for this enigmatic complex ranges loosely from the third century BC to the fourth century AD,[14] with signs of levelling the floor by back-filling the aisles and minor modifications that occurred at a much later date (Medieval to recent historic past).[15] The basis for the ancient dates are the pottery finds, which were both small in quantity and in the size of fragments that were recovered during the excavations of the site by the Italian Archaeological Mission to Malta between 1964 and 1967. Given that a George V coin was found in the material used to level the floor, the pottery is considered a secondary

[12] Buhagiar 1975, 167, examples of adjoining chapels include St Maddalena and St Leonards.

[13] *Contra* Bondì 1988, 271, who considered the area was left open and not roofed.

[14] Bonanno 2005, 340–341 BC. A summary of the Italian excavations of 1965 highlights the problematic issue of dating: "The later date of the sanctuary, the 1st century of the Christian era, is less puzzling as it is widely approximate and can oscillate a great deal," Cagiano de Azevedo, *et al.* 1966 (for 1965), 178. By the third year of excavation the situation was no clearer, the dates estimates were from the third century BC to fourth century AD, based entirely on secondary deposition of small pottery fragments, "alas, all of them (pottery sherds) come from transported earth which was most probably carried here from an area unrelated to the sanctuary," Cagiano de Azevedo, *et al.* 1967 (for 1966), 133.

[15] Buhagiar 1988, 74.

deposit imported to the site in the fill and in reality it may be more misleading than informative in fixing a date for the complex. More telling is the mortar used to smooth and level sections of the rock-cut benches in the long chamber as it was identified as a Roman form of plaster.

It has long been held that this site was late Punic or Hellenistic in date, but such rock-cut structures have no precedence in the Punic period. Ras il-Wardija is a thoroughly unique site in the archipelago and other than venturing to identify it as some form of sacred precinct (a nymphaeum),[16] the excavators assumed from the outset that in Ras il-Wardija they had a Punic site[17] and some graffiti was tenuously compared to examples in other Punic contexts.[18] An alternative identification, and one which has not been made before, is that Ras il-Wardija was a mithraeum. As such, a realistic estimate for the likely time span of this mithraeum is from the late first to early second through to the fourth century AD.

It is a site that is much eroded, especially since it was exposed through excavation, but significant features do survive that have some bearing on its ancient function. Possible lamp niches in the wall of the chamber[19] suggest that light was needed and if no other structure was built there, then they might imply night time rituals. The Cave may have been concealed — becoming an inner sanctum — by an additional structure built to abut the cliff face (Fig. 56). Traces of this Long Chamber floor have left scars on the rock; a screen may also have divided the two areas (for remains of the screen, see Fig. 58, lower left corner). Lamplight was needed because the whole complex was probably closed. Beck has argued that some mithraea were oriented to allow shafts of light from the rising or setting sun to fall on designated points inside the chamber.[20] Although there is no way of now determining this possibility for Ras il-Wardija, the buildings are roughly aligned on north-south (Long Chamber) and east-west (Cave) axes. Considering the geographic location of the site, there would have been no

[16] Cagiano de Azevedo, *et al.* 1965 (for 1964); Cagiano de Azevedo, *et al.* 1966 (for 1965); Cagiano de Azevedo, *et al.* 1967 (for 1966); Bozzi, *et al.* 1968 (for 1967).

[17] Bozzi, *et al.* 1968 (for 1967), 113–115.

[18] Buhagiar 2007, 15.

[19] Cagiano de Azevedo, *et al.* 1966 (for 1965), pl. 77:2, a lamp niche was positioned high on the western wall between the niches (near Fig. 55:15).

[20] Beck 1984, 364–365.

interruptions to the passage of sunlight. Because rock-cut Aisles 1 and 2 were preserved in such good condition,[21] this might indicate that for much of their existence, they were within a roofed chamber.[22]

Other shallow, rock-cut wall lines would appear to be the footings of an Exterior Compound wall running roughly north-south (and perhaps angling to the east in the northern sector). The entrance to the Exterior Compound might have stood inline with Aisle 2 as it ran from the inner sanctum (the Cave) to the break in the western bench (at point Fig. 55:8). A shallow, rectangular basin in the rock wall line of the Exterior Compound (Fig. 55:12) could have served as a socket for a larger cultic image or perhaps a pillar that formed part of a gate (Fig. 55). The break in the western bench is likely to be the main entrance to the Long Chamber building (Fig. 55:8) and here two larger and two small holes either side may have been postholes for the door (Fig. 55:13–14); the mere presence of a doorway strongly suggests that the Long Chamber was closed by walls. Another rectangular socket was cut in the southern jamb of the entrance (Fig. 55:17), which could have served as the foundation for a doorjamb or a socket for another cultic stela.[23] A possible second entrance could have been located at the north end of the building where the bedrock had been smoothed (Fig. 55:9).[24] If the break in the centre of the western bench (Fig. 55:8) was an entrance, then those who approached would have to step down into the Aisle 1 of the building. At the northern end, the bedrock falls away to a stepped ledge and beyond this, sheer drops to the sea (Figs 53–54).[25] There can be no doubt that in overall choice of site, Ras-il-Wardija would have satisfied the desire to be in an evocative natural setting close to water. Views from here toward adjoining rugged coastlines, over the

[21] The photographs in the reports clearly indicate the excellent condition of the features cut in the floor, see Cagiano de Azevedo, *et al.* 1965 (for 1964); Cagiano de Azevedo, *et al.* 1966 (for 1965); Cagiano de Azevedo, *et al.* 1967 (for 1966); Bozzi, *et al.* 1968 (for 1967).

[22] No roofing material was mentioned in the excavation reports, but given the exposed nature of the site and the intensive re-use of materials evident in the dry stone walls of the island, the possibility that the site was roofed over cannot be discounted.

[23] Cagiano de Azevedo, *et al.* 1966 (for 1965), pl. 86, 90:1 (right), 91:2.

[24] Cagiano de Azevedo, *et al.* 1966 (for 1965), pl. 93:1–2, the rock was quite smoothed, but is now very eroded and rough.

[25] Cagiano de Azevedo, *et al.* 1966 (for 1965), pl. 93:3.

expanse of the Mediterranean and to Malta in the south are spectacular (Fig. 54).[26]

Water accumulated at the site in a deep pool or cistern located to the south of the compound and the floor of the cistern was accessed by 10 steps cut down one side (Figs 55, right; 59),[27] as well as in a bell-shaped pit with rectangular opening (Fig. 60)[28] and possibly in eleven small basins found at the site.[29]

A primary reason for identifying the complex as a mithraeum lies in Aisles 1 and 2, which were cut to create benches or podia around all of the interior walls of the chambers.[30] A logical conclusion is that they functioned as seating for those participating in sacred Mithraic banquets; no other viable explanation has been offered to date. An estimate of at least 25 reclining people could be accommodated inside this mithraeum. Two altars each with two conical rock-cut pits were found: one in the south side of the Cave and one at the south-west end of the Long Chamber (Fig. 55:6 and 7). Cut into the Cave altar place was an additional small rectangular pit, which may have served as socket for a statue or plaque (Fig. 55:6).

Five substantial niches were cut into the walls of the Cave (Fig. 55:1–5; Fig. 58). Above the niches were traces of more elaborate lintels[31] and all of the niches may have been subdivided by shelves as indicated by slots cut midway in the sides, which may have taken wooded planks.[32] These niches may have held cult images and plaques depicting elements of the Mithraic mysteries as has been demonstrated at many of the off-shore cult centres. No central wall painting or relief

[26] Bonanno 2005, 89, has an aerial photograph demonstrating the spectacular cliff setting of Ras il-Wardija.

[27] For the early photographs of the cistern, see Cagiano de Azevedo, *et al.* 1967 (for 1966), fig. 12 the plan, pl. 58–59.

[28] The ball-shapes cistern, see Cagiano de Azevedo, *et al.* 1967 (for 1966), fig. 11 the plan, pl. 56–57.

[29] Cagiano de Azevedo, *et al.* 1967 (for 1966), 134, pl. 60:1–4, for some of the rock-cut basins.

[30] Even the Italian excavators suggested these were for use as seating, Cagiano de Azevedo, *et al.* 1966 (for 1965), 178.

[31] Cagiano de Azevedo, *et al.* 1966 (for 1965), pl. 77: 2, 78:1–2, 79:1, the lintels are very eroded, but still apparent over the top of the niches.

[32] The shelving grooves and other minor holes cut into the walls, may not be original and could date to the more recent re-use of the cave, see Buhagiar 1988, 73–74.

of the tauroctony survives. Some rather sketchy, naïve carvings in the walls of the cave (at Fig. 55:5, 15 and 16) can be likened to the depictions of Mithra emerging from the rock (the so-called 'rock-birth') with arms held up (Figs 30–32). These have variously been interpreted as meaningless graffiti, signs of Tanit[33] and Christian crosses.[34]

So little remains of another freestanding building on the lower terrace, at the cliff edge, that we can only speculate about its function (Fig. 57, foreground; Fig. 61). An exterior altar with two pits cut in the stones and roughly hewn blocks placed in a regular rectangular plan suggest that this, too, served a religious function.[35] Painted plaster fragments on both interior and exterior were found and it has been suggested that a lack of roofing material may indicate the structure was open to the air,[36] although the absence of most of the walls of this structure may indicate that such building material simply did not survive. This may have been a Punic temple, and as such was the first construction on the site. Temples with altars near the entrance of the main chambers is a Punic characteristic that can be seen at Tas-Silġ,[37] Kition (Cyprus)[38] among other sites.[39]

In many respects, the complex at Ras il-Wardija bears a strong resemblance in ground plan — some internal features and general cliff face setting — to a 'grotto' in Cyrene (Libya) called the Cave of the Priest, which Barnett suggested might reflect Mithraic or perhaps some other, unspecified mystery cult (Fig. 51).[40] Confirmation, however, comes in two fragments of Mithraic sculptures that were found nearby.[41] A basin in the centre of the cave was filled by a system of

[33] Bonanno 2005, 89. I have also referred in the past to one engraving in the niche on the eastern wall as that of Tanit, but in hindsight and considering the other Mithraic features of the site, I think Mithra is being represented.

[34] Cagiano de Azevedo, *et al.* 1966 (for 1965), pls 77:2, 78:1, a cross can be seen near the lamp niche may have been made at a later date; Buhagiar 2007, 15.

[35] Cagiano de Azevedo, *et al.* 1967 (for 1966), 134.

[36] Buhagiar 1988, p.76.

[37] Ciasca 1993, 228, fig. 1, who discusses Altar 45, "The sacrificial place closely connected to the temple and perfectly aligned with the centre of the concave front [remains of a prehistoric building] is the remains of structure *45*."

[38] Ciasca 1993, 232.

[39] Bondì 1988, 248 ff.

[40] Barnett in Wright 1957, 303.

[41] Barnett in Wright 1957, 304; see Vermaseren 1956, vol. 1, §106, §107, for the listing of the Mithraic sculptures from Cyrene, with bibliography.

water channels, which Barnett thought out of kilter with the usual mithraea;[42] yet, as already noted, others have indicated that nearby springs are often features near irrefutable mithraea. Such water installations do occur in mithraea, notably at Capua (Italy), discussed below. Hesitancy to accept that the Mithraic cult is manifest in the cliff face chamber in Cyrene is perhaps due to the dominance of the substantial temple dedicated to Apollo standing before it.[43] Considering the well-recognised syncretism between solar divinities, Mithra and Apollo included,[44] then it is not unexpected that traces of the Mysteries of Mithra were found at the site. Given the presence of the second southern temple at Ras il-Wardija, there may also have been a synchronism with Punic worship that lingered in Malta, perhaps an association with Baal Melqart or another of Baal's many guises.[45]

If the Cyrene cave, in essence, is a mithraeum, then there would be grounds for broadening the definition of characteristics of mithraea. While I am aware of the circularity of the argument, to then point to Ras il-Wardija as *ergo* a mithraeum, we are still faced with these two similar and enigmatic sites that do bear elements in keeping with unequivocal mithraea (namely cave setting, podia, central aisle, wall niches, altars, water supply and possible traces of Mithraic iconography). Scholars do recognise that there are regional variations in lay out and design of mithraea[46] and these cliff face grottos may reflect a southern Mediterranean variant.

The mithraeum in Capua has other similarities to the plan of the Ras il-Wardija site. Here benches flank the walls of the cult room (Fig. 52:1–2, 3–4) and of particular note is an adjoining long chamber (*vestibulum*) that is set at right angles (Fig. 52). A water basin (Fig. 52:5) and well with associated pipes (Fig. 52:6) were also fitted into the bench areas. A channel was cut at the front of the

42 Barnett in Wright 1957, 303–304.

43 See Wright 1957, fig. 1, general plan that illustrates rock-cut baths, water channels and a street to the south east of the chamber.

44 Clauss 1992, 155–156, lists sites where Apollo is invoked in inscriptions in connection with Mithra: Vindovala (at Hadrian's wall, Rudchester); Whitley Castle (Alston, Northumberland). Beck 2006, 222, one of Apollo's names included Mithra; see also pp. 230–231, for the Apollo Mithras Helios Hermes connection in reference to the Sun and to the planet Mercury.

45 Cagiano de Azevedo, *et al.* 1966 (for 1965), 179.

46 Clauss 2000, 42 *ff.*

podium against the back wall of the cult room (Fig. 52:7) and this channel fed water into the well. This mithraeum was well-adorned with unmistakable cult paintings.[47]

One final aspect, which has been mentioned in the publications concerning Ras il-Wardija, but with little detail given, is that on the crest of the hill under which the rock-cut sanctuary was made, were traces of other structures.

> It [Ras il-Wardija] extends over a large area from the terrace below the high rock, where there was a watch tower"[48]
> "the sounding done on the high rock — that is, on the highest part of the area where there are the ruins of a tower of uncertain date — has not shown clear signs of the presence of man in the old times, though certain cuts in the rock, possibly meant for the foundations of a building, could suggest ancient structures.[49]

A date for this tower was not given and no connection to the overall function of the site was made, however, Buhagiar notes the remains of a 'British semaphore signal station' is on the crest of the hill.[50] Could a Roman military post have been located in the region and the mithraeum formed the backdrop of the soldiers' religious practice? Certainly the fields around the site are scattered with late Punic and Romano-Punic pottery fragments and it is possible that a small settlement skirted the cliff tops. Not too distant from the Ras-il-Wardija complex, further east along the coast, is a large round well (possibly a sink hole) that is still filled with water that was reputedly a Roman water source. I do not know if this well has ever been investigated for any archaeological artefacts that might remain hidden beneath the water. Further east again is Xlendi Harbour well-known for marine archaeological finds of recent years, which clearly span from the Punic to Roman periods.[51]

[47] For the Capua mithraeum and its decorative panels, Vermaseren 1956, vol. 1, §180–199, 105–110, figs 50–60, see further references listed; Vermaseren 1971, for colour illustrations of the painted scenes.

[48] Cagiano de Azevedo, *et al.* 1966 (for 1965), 177.

[49] Cagiano de Azevedo, *et al.* 1966 (for 1965), 177.

[50] Buhagiar 1988, 72.

[51] Xlendi Harbour marine exploration came under the name 'Malta Project 2001', directed by Ayse Devrim Atauz. See brief discussion in Bonanno 2005, 255.

As to other possible mithraea in Malta, only tenuous suggestions can be made, but it is likely that the Mithraic cult has left some mark on the extensive burial grounds in Malta. In his comprehensive survey of the Late Roman period and Byzantine tombs and catacombs, Buhagiar noted that some tombs have more elaborate and unusual features perhaps more 'pagan' than Christian in character.

Binġemma Hypogeum 4 (Mġarr)

This artificial cave has no associated tombs although modifications such as tethering holes (Fig. 63:1–3, 5–8), an incised 'cross' (Fig. 63:at point 4) and a rock wall at the entrance may have been later additions; stone fragments in the debris on the floor suggest that the site had also been quarried.[52] Wide rock-cut benches still line the northern, western and southern corners and may have once extended further around the walls. Buhagiar is correct in dismissing the suggestion made by Lewis that these once formed *stibadia* (or *agape* tables).[53] It is more likely that they were seating for Mithraic gatherings. This is supported by the well-cut, arched niche in the rear wall (125 cm from the floor, 35 × 83 × 70 cm in size) towards the east corner into which a tethering hole has been cut probably when the chamber ceased to function as a mithraeum (Fig. 63:2); another niche that probably served as shelf for pottery was cut into the northwest wall. In addition, a number of lamp niches were cut into the walls. These surviving features strongly suggest a Mithraic function for this cave.

Binġemma Hypogeum 18 (Mġarr)

This complex is unlikely to have ever served as a mithraeum, but a cult follower may have been laid to rest there as seven lamp niches cut in a line above one tomb (Fig. 62:2).[54] As noted, quantities of seven have special significance in the Mithraic cult as do lamps, torches and light generally in reference to this solar deity and some mithraea are fitted with seven steps symbolising the seven planets — Saturn, Sol,

[52] Buhagiar 1986, 278, Hypogeum 4; Buhagiar 2007, 101, fig. 104.
[53] Buhagiar 1986, 278; Lewis 1977, 146.
[54] Buhagiar 1986, 285, fig. 89:1 (= Fig. 62:2).

Luna, Jupiter, Mars, Venus and Mercury — the stages of initiation and the passage of the soul through seven gates.[55] The seven lamp niches above the tomb may have some relevance in this regard.[56]

Binġemma Hypogeum 26 (Mġarr)

The central chamber of this complex is described as spacious (H 176 cm). Along the west and east walls are rock-cut benches (Fig. 64). Tomb 1 is accessed through a window door above the bench, but of note is that the entrance "is recessed in an arched frame" and of the entrance to Tomb 3, Buhagiar writes, it "has a similar window-entrance but the framing arch is more nobly proportioned."[57] It is possible that these two arched doorways were originally arched niches, the latter in the rear wall — as is seen in a number of instance — is the more elaborate, undoubtedly as it was a focal point upon entering and probably both niches functioned as alcoves for Mithraic cult objects.

Għar San Anard (vicinity of Wied Liemu, Rabat)

Of this site Buhagiar indicates that it was "a transformed natural cave of unknown antiquity" with a "rock-cut bench along the south wall [that] may be a relic of the original arrangement."[58] Much of its current appearance reflects fifteenth century alterations. Of interest, too, is a second cave from which a natural spring flows; its walls were embellished with graffiti of crosses.

Għar San Niklaw (near Mellieħa)

Għar San Niklaw is a cave that is situated high on the hillside overlooking the sea (Fig. 65). Although one section was possibly a functioning church up to the 1500s (Fig. 66:C), the cave was modified with dry stone walls for use as a habitation for people and their

[55] Vermaseren 1963, 138–162. Ferber 1971, 3–32, draws attention to Goodenough's argument that the seven steps leading to the Beth She'arim shrine, finds a parallel in the Mithraic shrine at Dura Europos among other signs of syncretism in the early Christian era (p. 12); see Goodenough 1953, vol. 1, 93, for the discussion.

[56] Buhagiar 1984, 21, note that another tomb has eight lamp holes and it may simply be reading too much into these occurrences.

[57] Buhagiar 1986, 291, Hypogeum 26.

[58] Buhagiar 2007, 100, fig. 118:b.

livestock.[59] It has traces of plaster and some fugitive red ochre paintwork that is thought to be Christian.[60] Significantly, in one wall of an area that K. Buhagiar describes as an 'apse-like recess' (Fig. 66:E) were seven lamp niches.[61] The symbolic value of seven within Mithraic practice has already been discussed. Other features are worthy of note in this regard. These are the shallow rectangular pit and channel cut into the floor as well as rock-cut benches against the cave walls into which troughs have been cut probably at a later date (Fig. 66 in area D).

Għar ta' Ibrudan (region of Rdum tal-Lunzjata, south west of Rabat)

At l-Għar ta' Ibrudan, a cave site consisting of three large areas that, it has been argued, served as a refuge during times of economic crisis at various times during the late Roman period.[62] Small rectangular lamp niches were cut in the walls of the complex and in other areas natural rock fissures lit the spaces. Here, late Roman (third to fifth century AD) coarse wares were found by Virzì Hägglund in sondages dug in 1972.[63] Although little has been written on the site, the pottery fragments are of the right chronological period to suggest further investigation of the site for any signs of Mithraic cult practices.[64]

Mellieħa Cave (below the rock-cut sanctuary of the Virgin, Mellieħa)

Buhagiar notes that the Mellieħa region has numerous rock-cut caves. One in particular is described as,

> Another cave 100 feet below [that is below the Sanctuary of the Virgin] may also have been a medieval church, though three limestone statues with strange graffiti are possibly pre-Christian.[65]

Again, the non-Christian appearance of the site is suggestive and the site warrants further investigation.

[59] Buhagiar 1975, 164–166.
[60] Buhagiar (K.) 1997, 133.
[61] Buhagiar (K.) 1997, 134
[62] Virzì Hägglund 1976–1977, 398.
[63] Virzì Hägglund 1976–1977, 396–399.
[64] Buhagiar 1983, 17, after Luttrell 1979, 461. Also mentioned in Messina 1989, 113, n. 12.
[65] Buhagiar 1975, 166, n. 17.

Salina Hypogea (St Paul's Bay)

While the catacombs or hypogea at Salina site are clearly the current dominant feature (Fig. 67:1), aspects of the forecourt around which Hypogea 1–4 are situated may have some relevancy in the quest to identify traces of Mithraic practice in Malta. The site lies in the north of the island near The Annunciation of the Virgin church in the region where the disciple Paul was reputedly shipwrecked. The forecourt of the catacombs is the area of interest, notable for its regular squarish plan with right-angled corners (L 8 m, W 4 m; Fig. 68:2). It is thought that the rectangular space was partially roofed over and that the walls were originally higher; it was possibly made private by a built front wall and entrance.[66] Like so many of the ancient monuments in Malta, these remains have felt the negative impact of more recent modifications due to field demarcation, quarrying and land development.[67] Lamp niches suggest that the complex was roofed over or possibly the area was used for night time rituals.[68]

Excavations were conducted at the site by L. J. Upton Way and his account of the work appeared in the *Times of Malta* in 1937.[69] He was struck by the nature of the open area off which the catacombs had been cut, judging it as a kind of amphitheatre for people to gather in commemoration for the deceased. In the north-west corner one rock-cut bench has survived. The entrance has two channels dug parallel to each other down the length of the 'entrance corridor'.[70]

Of note is the indistinct carved standing figures in a nearby hypogeum (Hypogeum 5) at the site (Fig. 29), which may depict Mithraic iconography, including a possible bust of Sol Invictus or a fire altar (see Part 1).[71]

Santa Caterina and Santa Maria (Tal-Baqqari, near Żurrieq)

Archaeological remains of some significance are associated with this site (Fig. 69). The folklore surrounding the paired structures and the reputed finds associated with them could be quite significant. Nearby is

66 Buhagiar 1984, 3.
67 Buhagiar 1984, 1–3.
68 Buhagiar 1984, 3, n. 15.
69 See Buhagiar 1984 and 1986, for the history of archaeological investigation of the Salina Hypogea; Upton Way 1937.
70 Buhagiar 1986, 140.
71 Musgrave 1979, 88–89.

an unfinished Punic grave[72] and also, from deep in Malta's prehistory, are the remains of megalithic blocks that date to the Temple Period.

Murray excavated the adjoining buildings in the 1920s[73] and she records that some folklore concerning the discovery of a golden bull at the site[74] and the location name has some association with cows or cow herders.[75] At the time, its date was only estimated from pre-Roman,[76] to Christian times. Murray toyed with possibility that it was a 'heathen shrine' later adapted to Christian worship.[77] An apse at the eastern end of the southern structure, Santa Maria, may have been a later addition to an original square plan.[78] Torba coated the floors of both buildings.

A cistern was located close to the buildings; water was a significant factor in mithraea of the Roman period, although Murray thought it to be of much later date (Medieval or later).[79]

Saint Peter's (Tat-Tarġa, near Naxxar)

The natural cave is approximately oval in shape. Some 7.50 m wide and 5.10 m in depth; traces of painted wall plaster were evident.[80]

Tal-Minsija (near Msieraħ)

Tal-Minsija is a cave left largely in its natural state and used as a church.[81]

Tal-Għolja (Siġġiewi)

Although tradition only suggested that this site functioned as a Christian sanctuary, Buhagiar argues that it was a habitation site[82], but it might warrant further investigation as a Mithriac centre.

72 Murray 1923, vol. 1, 18.
73 Murray 1923, vol. 1, 16–20, pl. 5; discussed in Buhagiar 1975, 164–165, fig. 6.
74 Murray 1923, vol. 1, 2, 16.
75 Wettinger 2000, 18.
76 Zammit recorded in Murray 1923, 17; Buhagiar 2007, 107, fig. 136.
77 Murray 1923, vol. 1, 17.
78 Murray 1923, vol. 1, 17–18.
79 Murray 1923, vol. 1, 18.
80 Buhagiar 1975, 166, n. 19.
81 Buhagiar 1975, 164.
82 Buhagiar 1975, 164, n. 11.

Ta'Żuta (Siġġiewi)

Tradition identifies this cave site as a Christian church, although Buhagiar argues that there is no proof of this.[83] Trump writes of the cave,

> The niches may have been cut to hold Roman cremation urns, making it a columbarium.[84]

Equally, it can be argued that the niches served as shelving in what might have been a mithraeum. Despite the site being devoid of ancient deposits due to more recent disturbances, the antiquity of the rock-cut recesses was not doubted by either scholar.

URBAN SETTING

Close proximity from one mithraeum to another such as in the case of the possible sites in Rabat does find parallel in other locations and is a result of the restricted membership of the cult group itself[85] and small, private places of worship (Fig. 70). These factors resulted in the proliferation of groups and their temples. The well-known and numerous mithraea found in Ostia (Italy) are described by Laeuchli,

> In their distribution and construction, the mithraea of Ostia are an integral part of the city. They are not superimposed foreign sanctuaries. They may have been so, certainly, in terms of their iconographic content, but they were not so in terms of their structures and integration into neighbourhoods and blocks. We find mithraea in all those buildings typical for such a city where granaries, warehouses, baths, apartment blocks, private homes and rich villas, rooms, storefronts, and lararia, odd spaces were converted into sanctuaries. The mithraea are not limited to any one region or even to a certain section of the city, but are found almost everywhere.[86]

Because there are no unequivocal mithraea with clear iconographic elements, religious paraphernalia or cult statues left *in situ* in Malta,

[83] Buhagiar 1975, 164, n. 11.
[84] Trump 1972, 121.
[85] St Agatha's catacombs and church complex in Buhagiar 1986, 94–146.
[86] Laeuchi 1968, 81–82.

one can only speculate that certain architectural elements that have survived are fossilised remnants of former mithraea. The sites that are discussed below, which may represent mithraea in urban settings in Malta probably reflect an *ad hoc* appearance of local sanctuaries in much the same way as they did in Ostia.

The 'Primary School' Hypogeum 1 (Ħal Pilatu, Rabat)

A catacomb was found during the construction of a primary school in Rabat in the late nineteenth century; it is preserved under the school (Figs 71–72) and can still be accessed.[87] Several steps lead down to Chamber I (3.20 × 2.03 m) and from this room, the squarish Chamber II (2.43 × 2.28 m) can be reached.[88] Benches that line all of the walls have been cut (probably at a later date) in order to construct the galleries and into three of the benches, small graves have also been made (Fig. 72:i–iii). The chambers are not very deep into the rock and Caruana points out that one of the extensions had to be sunk further down into the bed rock (Fig. 72:at door 6). As has been observed for other such chambers, the arched niche[89] in the rear wall (opposite the original entrance; Fig. 72:door 3) has been cut with some care and probably once formed a cultic niche only to be breached to form a door when the complex was converted into a catacomb. By contrast, the other door tops were less impressive (Fig. 72:doors 2 and 4), which does suggest that the complex had originally served quite a different function.

Both Caruana and Buhagiar saw Chamber II as serving as a place of assembly, although arguing that this involved some form of funerary ritual.[90] Significantly the latter suggested that this complex probably dated to a "pre-Christian culture."[91] Cutting the benches and making graves in the top of others, however, suggest that seating was not a priority for those who later converted the chambers into catacombs.

87 Caruana 1898, 91, pl. 23; Buhagiar 1986, 168–169.

88 Caruana 1898, Chamber B, pl. 23, fig. 1.

89 Buhagiar 1986, 169, draws attention to Vassallo's original plan of the catacomb on which 'arcuato' had been written in pencil by the surveyor.

90 Caruana 1898, 91; Buhagiar 1986, 169.

91 Buhagiar 1986, 169.

Saint Agatha's Hypogeum 7 (Rabat)

Nestled into an extensive complex of catacombs at the site of St Agatha's Museum and church complex, is a section identified as Hypogeum 7 (Figs 73–74).[92] This squarish, large room was originally accessed by its own individual entrance in its western wall and the complex lies on an east-west axis.[93] A remnant low bench survives that was cut with a child's grave. This grave as well as the additional chambers and graves (Fig. 74:1–4) may have been made at a later date. Measurements are not given of this room, but given the scale of the other chambers it must be slightly larger than 2.30 m square. The square plan and bench could indicate use as a mithraeum.

Saint Agatha's Hypogeum 13 (Rabat)

A similar argument can be made for another hypogeum in the St Agatha's complex (Fig. 76). Hypogeum 13 has some telling features. First, it is said to have been reached by several steps.[94] If this actually means seven steps, then this is a familiar hallmark of the cult.

This chamber is stuccoed with well-preserved, red-brown cement. The benches against the western and northern walls measure 55 by 48 cm.[95] The room drew the attention of Buhagiar as early as 1969, as it was clearly out of kilter with the usual catacomb structures.[96] The depiction of the east wall (Fig. 75:A) does show a small feature in the bottom right hand corner, but it does not appear to have been described (perhaps it is the remains of further bench [Fig. 75:A, iv]). In addition, Hypogeum 13 has a well-cut elongated niche (Fig. 75:A,

92 Buhagiar 1986, 71, fig. 17:a, general plan after Fr V. Camilleri (= Fig. 73),

93 Buhagiar 1986, 82, refers to this chamber as the antechamber and thought the bench was of interest.

94 Buhagiar 1986, 89.

95 Buhagiar 1986, 89, the benches "may have provided seating accommodation." The feature on the floor of the original chamber is a door plug that fitted into the doorway that was cut into the east wall.

96 Buhagiar 1969, 16–19, with detailed plans and sections on p. 17. "In the foregoing [discussion], my intention was merely to describe and therefore draw attention, to these two forgotten chambers at the extreme end of St. Agatha's catacombs. It would be presumptuous on my part to try to draw any conclusions but I feel sure that a proper investigation of them .... can shed much unsuspected light on the origin and evolution of this interesting complex of catacombs [1969, 19]."

iii) that may have accommodated a cult statue; like a number of examples discussed here, the large elongated niche was later cut through to form tombs. Beside it was a smaller and well-cut niche (Fig. 75:A, ii) that was thought to have served as a shelf for pottery and was not intended for use as a grave, hence it is likely to have been part of the original features.[97]

Saint Leonard's (Lunzjata Valley, bordering Rabat)

Traces of painted wall plaster were observed in this cave-church[98] and benches once bordered the walls of the chamber.[99] It may have originally served a Mithraic function

Saint Maria della Virtú (Rabat, Saint Dominic's Priory)

Although this site, described as a crypt, has a decorative door built in the fifteenth century, it gave access to a rock-cut chamber perhaps of greater antiquity (Fig. 77). Like the chapel of Saint Mary Magdalene, it has been argued that this chamber was formed by recutting a palaeochristian hypogeum, but in this case two pillars held the roof through which two skylights allowed light to enter. Significantly, this irregular, somewhat lobed area was accessed by several steps and it once had several altars (only one survived in the 1500s) as well as rock-cut benches.[100]

Saint Maria tal-Għar (Rabat)

Linked to Christian catacombs, this church also had stone benches that were around the interior walls. Its entrance was framed by stone columns and a marble lintel that was an architectural element re-used from a larger Roman monument.[101] The plan incorporated three apses

[97] Buhagiar 1986, 89, the smaller shelf was "probably intended to contain a small vase or some other pottery vessel."

[98] Buhagiar 1975, 166.

[99] Buhagiar 1975, 167.

[100] Buhagiar 2007, 99, after the manuscript by Dusina (1575) and Abela's 1647 work (p. 47); Buhagiar 1986, 193–194, fig. 62:B.

[101] Buhagiar 1975, 167, the lintel it is suggested came from a "Roman composite entablature"; Buhagiar 2007, 57.

in which altars were placed. As for Saint Leonard's, the structure may have originally been a mithraeum.

Saint Mary Magdalene (near Saint Paul's Grotto, Rabat)

Continuous rock-cut benches (H 45 cm, W 92 cm) that lined the walls of this roughly circular chamber are suggestive; red, crushed pottery plaster coated its walls. Buhagiar noted that the site had additional side chambers and traces of tomb structures, the latter perhaps indicating that the site was "recut from a paleochristian hypogeum".[102] Features in the complex, namely a stone altar and a "mural meant to instil a fear of death" are intriguing, but obscure.[103]

Saint Paul's Grotto (Rabat)

The catacombs may have had some earlier history that hint at Mithraic traits. According to Buhagiar,

> St. Paul's Grotto, traditionally associated with Saints Paul, Luke and Trophimus, had a possibly medieval mural depicting St. Paul with upraised hand and a burning taper at his feet.[104]

The significant of a flame and figures with an arm held up are familiar to Mithraic iconography. The latter recalls the torch bearers who flank depictions of Mithra. The sacred quality of fire in this essentially eastern cult hails to back to Zoroastrianism and the tending of the perpetual and sacred fire is well-known. The cave has been altered considerably in recent history.[105]

Saint Paul-Saint Agatha area, Catacomb 6 (Rabat)

A number of independent catacombs are situated between St Paul's and St Agatha's catacombs. Within Catacomb 6 is a familiar pattern consisting of an entrance approached by a series of steps to a squarish antechamber leading to an inner chamber (Buhagiar's 'Extension II')

[102] Buhagiar 2007, 99, no plan is given of the site.

[103] Buhagiar 2007, 99, after a manuscript by Dusina 1575.

[104] A G. Zammit Maempel located an engraving of the painting, see Buhagiar 1975, 166, n. 23.

[105] Buhagiar 2007, 99, fig. 11, for a plan of the site.

flanked by benches 62 cm high and 37 cm wide (Fig. 78).[106] As Buhagiar states the room "may have served as a place of assembly" and was illuminated by several lamp niches (again if by several he means seven, then this is significant).[107] The complex was largely filled with debris when Buhagiar made his comprehensive study of the catacombs in Malta, but he does illustrate the entrance with arched frame to the chamber with benches (Fig. 78: section A–B).[108]

Saint Paul-Saint Agatha area, Catacomb 20 (Rabat)

Concerning Catacomb 20 (Fig. 79), Buhagiar notes at the outset that, "its Christian origin is doubtful."[109] Cut close to the surface than most catacombs, it is reached by a few steps that lead down to the large chamber (referred to as an 'antechamber' leading to two galleries of tombs). Significantly, low benches are located on all four walls and these were cut later to create the two galleries of tombs. The appearance that this chamber was meant for a ritual did not escape Buhagiar,

> ...the benches may have provided seating for the mourners assembled for the entombment ceremony.[110]

The bench at the entrance function as the final step down. Of particular interest are two rock-cut, shallow and rectangular depressions in the bench. One in the corner had a rebate edge (Fig. 79:b), a feature that suggests that this served as a socket for a cultic image; the second plain pit probably served a similar function.[111] Such features are known from other mithraea and can also be seen at Ras il-Wardija in Gozo (Fig. 55:6, 12, 17). An arched doorway in the wall opposite the entrance may have originally been a recess for another cult statue, but this wall and its features are not illustrated. It appears to have been the better of the two doors cut into the chamber leading to rock-cut galleries.[112]

[106] Buhagiar 1986, 105
[107] Buhagiar 1986, 105, fig. 27.
[108] Buhagiar 1986, 101.
[109] Buhagiar 1986, 138; Buhagiar 2007, 25.
[110] Buhagiar 1986, 138.
[111] Buhagair 1986, 138, their function was unknown, but he did draw a parallel to another example in the Tac-Caghqi hypogeum (1986, 189–190).
[112] Buhagiar 1986, 138–139.

Saint Paul-Saint Agatha area, Catacomb 22B (Rabat)

At least seven steps lead down to Catacomb 22 B although the original entrance is walled up. Two chambers have benches along one or more of the walls (Fig. 80:1, A, i–iii; Fig. 80:1, B, v and Fig. 80:2, f). These have been further cut, probably at some later date, to form children's graves (Fig. 80: 1, A, i–ii and B, v).[113] A 'cupboard-like recess' is located right of the entrance in Chamber B[114] with a further 'apsed pottery shelf' is located in the rear wall (Fig. 80:2b) above the entrance to a gallery. Three lamp niches (Fig. 80: 2, a, c, e) are cut in this wall. If these chambers began as rooms in a mithraeum, then Chamber A is likely to have been the main cult room and Chamber B a storeroom for cult utensils with its rock-cut shelves.[115] The door to the adjoining gallery (Fig. 80:2, g) and the cutting above it, which served as a child's grave (Fig. 80:2, d) are thus likely to be later modifications to the room.

Saint Vennera (near Saint Agatha's Catacombs, Rabat)

A rock-cut church through which a catacomb was reached was located in St Vennera. Although these can no longer be entered, they reputedly had a painting of person holding a flaming vessel, which is interpreted as St Vennera, but it might have been a Mithraic figure.[116]

Tac-Caghqi Secondary School — South-East Hypogeum (Tac-Caghqi, Rabat)

This hypogeum was investigated in 1952[117] and consisted of six burial chambers cut off a large hall that, it is argued here, may have been originally a mithraeum, based largely on the benches around the walls (Fig. 81:1–6),

113 Buhagiar 1986, 140–143.

114 Buhagiar 1986, 142, feature 25 in his chamber 'f'.

115 For multi-roomed mithraea with rooms used for utensil storage see, Vermaseren 1956 and 1960.

116 Abela 1647, Book I, not. iv, 46–47; Buhagiar 1986, 147.

117 Baldacchino 1954 (for 1951–1952), 1–3.

> Six rock-benches are cut along the walls of the hall. Their original purpose might have been to provide seating accommodation for the congregation assembled for the burial or libation rites but tombs for children were subsequently dug in four of them...[118]

Only one bench was left intact (Fig. 81:5). Bench 6 had a rectangular shaped shallow depression cut in the top (Fig. 81:6), which could have served to hold a cult statue — a feature seen in other locations.[119] It is clear that the chamber was meant for people to assemble and that this may have formed another cult centre in all likelihood dedicated to Mithra. An inscription in the complex was dated broadly between the second century BC and first century AD, but remained in use long after.[120]

Various fugitive traces of painted inscriptions and decorative features were observed, but whether they can be associated with Mithraic iconography (or Christian for that matter) is far from clear.[121] A painted palm tree motif (Fig. 39:3; Fig. 81:at point 3) in the main hall has been linked to Christian practice, but palms, as already discussed have a much wider application, including in Mithraic practice.[122]

Tal-Abbatija tad-Dejr — the Chapel, The Nativity of the Virgin (abutting the Tad-Dejr Catacombs, Rabat)

The chapel in the Abbatija tad-Dejr Hypogea complex (Fig. 82:1) has remnants of stone benches on two sides of the chamber that are likely to have spanned the length of the walls (Fig. 84:2).[123] This small, rock-cut structure is only 3 m by 2.70 m with an apse 120 cm deep by 180 cm across. The benches, small chamber with rock-cut pillars, stone basin (now lost) and rear wall apse (W 1.82 m, Dp 1.21 m) do fall into line with known mithraea. It was adorned with Christian frescos possibly in the fourteenth century.[124] Significant, however, is an incised

[118] Buhagiar 1986, 189.

[119] Buhagiar 1986, 189–190, other than suggesting that it might have served as an ossuary, Buhagiar could not explain the purpose of this feature.

[120] Buhagiar 2007, 25.

[121] Buhagiar 2007, 25, this complex is classed generally as 'pagan'.

[122] See Buhagiar 1986, 190.

[123] Buhagiar 1986, 208–211, fig. 67:B, point 'c'. Buhagiar 2007, 92, 99–100, fig. 115, for a more recent discussion of the site.

[124] Buhagiar 1975, pl. 14a.

palm frond on the south wall, which Buhagiar stated was of unknown date; as noted palms can be a Mithraic iconographic element.[125] The walled up original entrance may be relevant, perhaps sealed by early Christian elements in their eradication of Mithraic centres.

Tal-Abbatija — the Rectangle, or Oratory (the Tad-Dejr Catacombs, Rabat)

Located in the vicinity of the Chapel and Tad-Dejr catacomb, this chamber coined 'the Rectangle' may also have formed part of the Mithraic history of the site. Although badly damaged and reputedly quarried in the past, it is now open to the air. The site was probably once (partially?) roofed over and its plan is basically a rock-cut rectangular depression (Fig. 83). In the southern rear corner (Fig. 83:c), traces of a niche survive that was possibly arched at the top; it is likely to have served a cult purpose. Two rock-cut benches with tombs cut into the tops (presumably cut at a later date) have also survived (Fig. 83:a–b).[126]

Wignacourt Museum (Rabat)

In recent years, the network of catacombs and second world war, air raid shelters beneath Wignacourt Museum have been cleared of accumulated debris. One of the ancient chambers has rock-cut benches against each of the walls.[127]

[125] Buhagiar 1986, 211; Appendix III,. 416, no. 59. Other graffiti on the wall included a boat and a Latin cross.

[126] Buhagiar 1986, 212–213, fig. 67: A, D; Buhagiar 2007, 100, fig. 79.

[127] I was fortunate to be part of a small group who toured the subterranean chambers with Canon John Azzopardi.

CONCLUSIONS

The presence of Mithra and the mithraea on the islands opens up a new dimension to the history of the Maltese Archipelago in the early centuries of the first millennium AD. It may offer a long needed solution for features in the catacombs that have never sat comfortably with conventional thought on early Christianity. This was a time of religious experimentation and development often characterised by mystery doctrines and secret rites. Some overlap in religious expression, funerary practice and architectural remains, could be expected.[1] Transference of ritual practices between different religious contexts has numerous parallels: for example, Easter eggs celebrating Christ's resurrection, or the origins of the red and white suit of Saint Nicholas that can be traced back ironically to the shadowy beginnings of the Magi, Zoroastrianism and the use of the hallucinogenic narcotic *hoama*,[2] as well as the transference of the celebration of Mithra's birthday on the 25th December to that of Christ's. The links between Mithraism and Christianity have been the subject of numerous studies and the issues they raise concerning theology, community and the vacuum created, by what Laeuchi refers to as religious 'bankruptcy' of Rome,[3] may have some relevancy to the evidence in Malta — a thesis in itself.

In the context of the Maltese Archipelago, as in all of the Roman territories, Mithraism took on differing characteristics probably influenced by local traditions. In Malta, an island that remained more Punic than Roman long after 218 BC, we can suggest that whether foreign elements — soldiers and officials — or local inhabitants aspiring to thrive within the Roman system, they drew inspiration from well-entrenched beliefs. A degree of symbiosis saw the iconography of Mithra merge with Apollo and Hercules, which had already formed

[1] Gates 1984, 167–168, indicates the there were many similarities between the mithraeum, synagogue and Christian chapel in Dura Europos despite the Roman conquest and colonisation in the second and third centuries AD.

[2] Sagona and Sagona (in press); Wasson 1968.

[3] For links between Christianity and Mithraism see, Laeuchli 1967, 85–105; Martin 1989; Clauss 2000, pp 168–172; Boyce and Grenet 1991, 440–446.

an overlay to older Phoenician-Punic worship of the dying and rising god, Baal-Melqart. Just as Astarte, was associated with Juno by the time Cicero berated Verres for the plunder of her temple at Tas-Silġ in Malta.[4]

There is enough evidence to indicate that devotees to Mithra were present in the Maltese Archipelago. One can only speculate as to the function of the few plaques that have survived in Malta, but it is highly likely that they were placed in the mithraea on the islands. Just as the funerary contexts may have preserved traces of Mithraic iconography, so other sites may have been created to serve those devoted to Mithra.

As the Mithraic cult in Malta has not been identified before, there may be some merit in looking again at other locations, those traditionally associated with early Christian belief, funerary contexts, or troglodyte dwelling. It is hoped that we have reached a point where elements of mithraic architectural design can be recognised in somewhat ambiguous contexts, or in structures that came to be dominated by Christian elements and subjected to later extensive modifications. Nestled in the heart of some complex catacomb systems may be the kernel of how they began, not as funerary sites, but as religious places of worship dedicated to an enigmatic deity, whose origins began in the highlands of the Eastern Turkey and Iranian Plateau. Just as the *stibadia* and certain iconography are accepted as Christian, we can now suggest that small, cave-like, subterranean chambers, sometimes with benches, lamp niches and well-cut often arched alcoves were made by followers of Mithra. This is a new chapter in Maltese archaeological history, one that may lead to a greater understanding of what the islands were experiencing in the first centuries of the first millennium. It may suggest a certain religious tension and cultural flux, as the local inhabitants adjusted to life under the Roman domination. Perhaps there is even a degree of survival strategy in the religious adaptations that took place.

[4] Cicero Book II, XLVI §102–XLVII §105; Ciasca 1993, 226.

BIBLIOGRAPHY

Abela, G. F. 1647. *Della Descrittione di Malta Isola nel Mare Siciliano, con le sue Antichita, ed altre Notitie*. Melitensia Book Club, no. 1 (1984). Valletta: Midsea Books.

Ashby, T. 1915. "Roman Malta." *Journal of Roman Studies* 5:23–80.

Baldacchino, J. G. 1954. "Catacombs at Rabat." *Annual Report on the Working of the Museum Department 1951–1952.* Malta: Government Printing Office, pp. 1–3.

Barbaro, C. A. 1794. *Degli Avanzi d'Alcuni Antichissini Edifici Scvoperti in Malta l'Anno 1768*. Malta.

Beck, R. 1984. "The Rock-cut Mithraea of Arupium (Dalmatia)." *Phoenix* 38(4):356–371.

—, 1998. "The Mysteries of Mithras: A New Account of their Genesis." *The Journal of Roman Studies* 88:115–128.

—, 2000. "Ritual, Myth, Doctrine, and Initiation in the Mysteries of Mithras: New Evidence from a Cult Vessel." *Journal of Roman Studies* 90:145–180.

—, 2004. *Beck on Mithraism. Collected Works with New Essays*. Aldershot (Hampshire): Ashgate.

—, 2006. *The Religion of the Mithras Cult in the Roman Empire. Mysteries of the Unconquered Sun*. Oxford: Oxford University Press.

Bishop, M. C. and Coulston, J. C. N. 2006. *Roman Military Equipment: from the Punic Wars to the Fall of Rome*, second edition. Oxford: Oxbow.

Bonanno, A. 1977. "Distribution of Villas and Aspects of Some of the Maltese Economy in the Roman Period." *Journal of the Faculty of Arts* (Malta) 6(4):73–81.

—, 1992. *Roman Malta. The Archaeological Heritage of the Maltese Islands*. Rome: Giuseppe Castelli and Charles Cini.

—, 1996. "Egyptian Iconography in Ancient Maltese Art." *Treasures of Malta* 2(3):43–47.

—, 2005. *Malta: Phoenician, Punic and Roman*. Malta's Living Heritage Series. Malta: Midsea Books.

Bondì, S. F. 1988. "City Planning and Architecture," in *The Phoenicians*, edited by S. Moscati, pp. 248–283. Milan: Bompiani.

Borg, V. and Rocco, B. 1972. "L'Ipogeo di Tac-Caghki a Malta: Part I–II Monumento Funerario," in *Sicilia Archaeologica — Rassegna Periodica di Studi, Notizie e Documentazione*, edited by E. P. T. di Trapani, vol. 5, nos 18–19–20 (June-September-December), pp. 61–74.

Boyce, M. and Grenet, F. 1991. *A History of Zoroastrianism. Volume 3, Zoroastrianism under Macedonian and Roman Rule*. Leiden: Brill.

Bozzi, C., Cagiano de Azevedo, M., Caprino, C., Ciasca, A., Davico, A., Del Monaco, R., Garbini, G., Pugliese, B. and Rossignani, M. P. 1968. *Missione Archeologica Italiana a Malta–Rapporto Preliminare della Campagna, 1967.* Rome: Università degli studi di Roma, Istituto di studi del Vicino Oriente.

Brandon, S. G. F. 1975. "The Idea of the Judgement of the Dead in the Ancient Near East," in Mithraic Studies. *Proceedings of the First International Congress of Mithraic Studies,* edited by J. R. Hinnells, pp. 470–478. Manchester: Manchester University Press.

Bres, O. 1816. *Malta Antica Illustrata co' Monumenti et coll'Istoria. Militensia Book Club, no. 4, Facsimile Edition*. Valletta: Midsea Books.

Buhagiar, K. 1997. "The San Niklaw Cave-settlement." *Melita Historica* 12(2):131–137.

Buhagiar, M. 1969. "Report on Two Interesting Chambers in St. Agatha's Catacombs and a Number of Early 16th Century Carved Stone Blocks in the Museum of the Missionary Society of St. Paul." *Din L-Art Helwa Quarterly* (Malta) 1(1):13–24.

—, 1975. "Medieval Churches in Malta", in *Medieval Malta: Studies on Malta before the Knights,* A. T. Luttrell, pp. 163–180. London: British School at Rome.

—, 1976. "The Annunciation Church at Ħal Millieri," in *Ħal Millieri: a Maltese Casale, its Churches and Paintings*, edited by A. Luttrell, pp. 69–89. Malta: Midsea Books.

—, 1983. "Mediterranean Architecture: Medieval Cave Dwellings and Rock-cut Churches in Malta." *Atrium* (Mediterranean and Middle East Architecture) 3:17–22.

—, 1984. "The Salina Bay Hypogea at St. Paul's Bay." *Melita Historica* 9(1):1–18.

—, 1986. *Late Roman and Byzantine Catacombs and Related Burial Places in the Maltese islands*. Oxford: BAR International Series 302.

—, 1988. "Two Archaeological Sites — Ras ir-Raħeb, Malta, and Ras il-Wardija, Gozo." *Melita Historica* 10(1):69–87.

—, 1997. "The St. Paul Shipwreck Controversy an Assessment of the Source Material," in *Proceedings of History Week 1993,* edited by M. Buhagiar, pp. 181–213. Malta: The Malta Historical Society.

—, 2001. "Early Post-Muslim Art and Architecture in Malta: the Latin Imprint." *Treasures of Malta* 8(1):15–21, 115.

—, 2007. *The Christianisation of Malta. Catacombs, Cult Centres and Churches in Malta to 1530.* Oxford: BAR International Series no. 1674.

Busuttil, G., Cagiano de Azevedo, M., Ciasca, A., D'Andria, G., Del Monaco, R. Guzzo Amadasi, M. G., Pugliese, B. O. and Rossignani, M. P. 1969.

Missione Archeologica Italiana a Malta. Rapporto Preliminare della Campagna 1968, Consiglio Nazionale della Ricerche, Centro di Studio per la Civiltà Fenicia e Punica. Rome: Presso l'Istituto di Studi Vicino Oriente dell'Università di Roma.

Cagiano de Azevedo, M. 1967. "Note su trovamenti vari," in *Missione Archeologica Italiana a Malta. Rapporto Preliminare della Campagna 1966*, by M. Cagiano de Azevedo, *et al.*, pp. 49–52. Rome: Istituto di Studi del Vicino Oriente, Università degli Studi di Roma, Centro di Studi Semitici.

Cagiano de Azevedo, M., Caprino, C., Ciasca, A., Coleiro, E., Davico, A., Garbini, G., Mallia, F. S., Marchi, G. P., Minganti, P., Moscati, S., Paribeni, E., Pugliese, B., Rossignani, M. P., Santa Maria Scrinari, V. and Stenico, A. 1965. *Missione Archeologica Italiana a Malta–Rapporto Preliminare della Campagna, 1964*. Rome: Centro di Studi Semitici, Istituto di Studi del Vicino Oriente, Università degli Studi di Roma.

Cagiano de Azevedo, M., Caprino, C., Ciasca, A., Coleiro, E., Davico, A., Garbini, G., Mallia, F. S., Moscati, S., Pugliese, B., Rossignani, M. P. and Tamassia, A. M. 1966. *Missione Archeologica Italiana a Malta–Rapporto Preliminare della Campagna 1965*. Rome: Istituto di Studi del Vicino Oriente, Università degli Studi di Roma.

Cagiano de Azevedo, M., Caprino, C., Ciasca, A., Coleiro, E., Davico, A., Garbini, G., Moscati, S., Pugliese, B., Rossignani, M. P., and Tamassia, A. M. 1967. *Missione Archeologica Italiana a Malta. Rapporto Preliminare della Campagna 1966*. Rome: Istituto di Studi del Vicino Oriente, Università degli Studi di Roma, Centro di Studi Semitici.

Cagiano de Azevedo, M., Caprino, C., Ciasca, A., D'Andria, F., Davico, A., Grottanelli, C., Guzzo Amadasi, M. G., Martinelli Coco, T. and Rossignani, M. P. 1972. *Missione Archeologica Italiana a Malta. Rapporto Preliminare della Campagna 1969*. Rome: Presso l'Istituto di Studi Vicino Oriente dell'Università di Roma, Consiglio Nazionale della Ricerche, Centro di Studio per la Civiltà Fenicia e Punica.

Cagiano de Azevedo, M., Caprino, C., Ciasca, A., D'Andria, F., Davico, A., Guzzo Amadasi, M. G. and Rossignani, M. P. 1973. *Missione Archeologica Italiana a Malta. Rapporto Preliminare della Campagna 1970*. Rome: Presso l'Istituto di Studi Vicino Oriente dell'Università di Roma, Consiglio Nazionale della Ricerche, Centro di Studio per la Civiltà Fenicia e Punica.

Camilleri, V. 1994. *St Agatha's Museum Rabat - Malta*. Malta: M.S.S.P.

Caruana, A. A. 1882. *Report on the Phoenician and Roman Antiquities in the Group of the Islands of Malta*. Malta: Government Printing Office.

—, 1898. *Ancient Pagan Tombs and Christian Cemeteries in the Islands of Malta Explored and Surveyed from the Year 1881 to the Year 1897*. Malta: Government Printing Office.

Ciasca, A. 1993 "Some Considerations Regarding the Sacrificial Precincts at Tas-Silġ." *The Journal of Mediterranean Studies* (Malta) 3(2):225–244.

Cicero 1967. *The Verrine Orations*, English translation by L. H. G. Greenwood, volume II, part 2, books III–V. London: William Heinemann.

Clauss, M. 1992. *Cultores Mithrae. Die Abhängerschaft des Mithraskultes.* Stuttgart.

—, 2000. *The Roman Cult of Mithras. The God and his Mysteries.* Translated by R. Gordon with additional bibliography by Gordon. Edinburgh: Edinburgh University Press.

Clermont-Ganneau, C. 1903. "Les Sépulcres à Fresques de Guigariche et le Culte de Mithra en Afrique." *Comptes-Rendus Académie des Inscriptions*, pp. 357–363.

Cumont, F. 1896 and 1899. *Textes et Monuments Figurés Relatifs aux Mystères de Mithra*, 2 volumes. Brussels: H. Lamertin. New York: Dover Publications.

—, 1956. *The Mysteries of Mithra.* Translated from the second revised French edition (1903) by T. J. McCormack. New York: Dover Publications.

Curtis, J. 1989. *Ancient Persia.* London: The British Museum.

Dalli, C. 2006. *Malta: the Medieval Millennium.* Malta's Living Heritage Series. Malta: Midsea Books.

Daniels, C. M. 1975. "The Role of the Roman Army in the Spread and Practice of Mithraism," in *Mithraic Studies. Proceedings of the First International Congress of Mithraic Studies*, edited by J. R. Hinnells, pp. 249–274. Manchester: Manchester University Press.

David, J. 2000. "The Exclusion of Women in the Mithraic Mysteries: Ancient or Modern?" *Numen* 47(2):121–141.

Delattre, R. P. 1898. "La Nécropole Punique Voisine de la Colline de Siant-Monique. Le Premier Mois des Fouilles Janvier 1898." *Cosmos*, pp. 1–21. (Paris: E. Petithenry)

Ferber, S. 1971. "The Pre-Constantine Shrine of St. Peter: Jewish Sources and Christian Aftermath." *Gesta* 10(2):3–32.

Garbini, G., Moscati, S., Pennacchietti, F. A., Pugliese, B. and Scrinari, V. 1964. *Missione Archeologica Italiana a Malta. Rapporto Preliminare della Campagna 1963.* Rome: Università degli Studi di Roma, Centro di Studi Semitici, Istituto di Studi del Vicino Oriente.

Gates, M.-H. 1984. "Dura-Europos: A Fortress of Syro-Mesopotamian Art." *The Biblical Archaeologist* 47(3):166–181.

Goodenough, E. R. 1953–1968. *Jewish Symbols in the Greco-Roman Periods.* Bollingen Series vols 1–6. New York: Bollingen Foundation — Pantheon Books.

Gouder, T. C. 1973. "Baal Hammon in the Iconography of the Ancient Bronze Coinage of Malta." *Scientia*, a quarterly scientific review 36(3):1–16.

Guidobaldi, F. 1978. *Il Complesso Archeologico di S. Clemente. Clemente. Risultati degli Scavi più Recenti e Riesame dei Resti Architettonici*. Rome.

Helgeland, J. 1978. "Roman Army Religion," in *Aufstieg und Niedergang der Römischen Welt: Geschichte und Kultur Rom sim Spiegel der Neueren Forschung II*, edited by H. Temporini and W. Haase, pp. 1470–1505. Berlin and New York: Walter de Gruyter.

Hinnells, J. R., ed. 1975. *Proceedings of the First International Congress of Mithraic Studies*. Manchester: Manchester University Press.

Hock, A. D. 1932. "Cremation and Burial in the Roman Empire." *The Harvard Theological Review* 25(4):321–359.

Iles Johnston, S. 1992. "Riders in the Sky: Cavalier Gods and Theurgic Salvation in the Second Century A.D." *Classical Philology* 87(4):303–321.

Jackson, H. M. 1985. "The Meaning and Function of the Leon-Tocephaline in Roman Mithraism." *Numen* 32(fasc. 1):17–45.

Jones, P. and Pennick, N. 1997. *A History of Pagan Europe*. London and New York: Routledge.

Kane, J. P. 1975. "The Mithraic Cult Meal in its Greek and Roman Environment," in Mithraic Studies. *Proceedings of the First International Congress of Mithraic Studies*, edited by J. R. Hinnells, pp. 313–351 with discussion pp. 352–357. Manchester: Manchester University Press.

Kitzinger, E. 1960. "A Marble Relief of the Theodosian Period." *Dumbarton Oaks Papers* 14:17–42.

Laeuchli, S. 1967. "Christ and Mithra," in *Mithraism in Ostia. Mystery Religion and Christianity in the Ancient Port of Rome*, pp. 85–105. Illinouis: Northwestern University Press.

—, 1968. "Urban Mithraism." *The Biblical Archaeologist* 31(3):73–99.

Laeuchli, S. ed. 1967. *Mithraism in Ostia. Mystery Religion and Christianity in the Ancient Port of Rome*. Illinouis: Northwestern University Press.

Levi, D. 1944. "Aion." *Hesperia* 13(4):269–314.

Lewis, H. 1977. *Ancient Malta: A Study of its Antiquities*. Gerrards Cross, Bucks: Colin Smythe.

Liebeschuetz, J. H. W. G. 2006. *Decline and Change in Late Antiquity: Religion, Barbarians and their Historiography*. Aldershot: Ashgate Publishing.

Luttrell, A. 1979. "Malta Troglodytica: Ghar il-Kbir." *Heritage* (Encyclopedia of Maltese Culture and Civilization) 24:461–464.

Martin, L. H. 1989. "Roman Mithraism and Christianity." *Numen* 36(1):2–15.

Messina, A. 1989. "Trogloditismo Medievale a Malta." *Melita Historica* 10(2):109–120.

Miller, H. F. 1979. *The Iconography of the Palm in Greek Art: Significance and Symbolism*. PhD thesis, University of California, Berkeley. Ann Arbor – London: University Microfilms International.

Murray, M. A. 1923. *Excavations in Malta*, with a chapter by G. Caton Thompson. London: Bernard Quaritch.

Musgrave, G. H. 1979. *Friendly Refuge: a Study of St. Paul's Shipwreck and his Stay in Malta*. Sussex: Heathfield Publications.

Nicholson, O. 1995. "The End of Mithraism." *Antiquity* 69(no. 263):358–362.

Quasten, J. 1940. "Vetus Superstitio et Nova Religio" the Problem of Refrigerium in the Ancient Church of North Africa." *The Harvard Theological Review* 33(4):253–266.

Sagona, C. 2002. *The Archaeology of Punic Malta*. Louvain: Peeters.

Sagona, C. and Sagona A. (In press). "The Mushroom, the Magi and the Keen-sighted Seer," in *The Black Sea, Greece, Anatolia and Europe in the 1st Millennium BC*, studies dedicated to Prof. J. Bouzek, edited by G. R. Tsetskhladze. Colloquia Pontica series.

Sagona, C., Vella Gregory, I. and Bugeja, A. 2006. *Punic Antiquities of Malta and other Ancient Artefacts held in the Ecclesiastic and Private Collections, 2*. Ancient Near Eastern Studies, supplement 18. Louvain: Peeters.

Sammut, J. C. 2001. *Currency in Malta*. Malta: Central Bank of Malta.

Schreiber, J. 1967. "The Environment of Ostian Mithraism," in *Mithraism in Ostia. Mystery Religion and Christianity in the Ancient Port of Rome*, edited by S. Laeuchli, pp. 22–45. Illinois: Northwestern University Press.

Swinton, J. 1768. "Description of a Punic Coin Appertaining to the Isle of Gozo, Hitherto Attributed to that of Malta, by the Learned. In a letter to Mathew Maty, M. D. Sec. R. S. from the Rev. John Swinton, B. D. F. R. S. Custos Archivorum of the University of Oxford, Member of the Academy Degli Apatisti at Florence, and of the Etruscan Academy of Cortona in Tuscany." *Philosophical Transactions* (for 1683–1775) 58:261–264.

Trump, D. 1972. *Malta: An Archaeological Guide*. London: Faber and Faber.

Upton Way, L. J. 1937. "Catacombs near Salina Bay." *The Times of Malta* 29.6.1937.

Ustinova, Y. 1999. *The Supreme Gods of the Bosporan Kingdom: Celestial Aphrodite and the Most High God*. Religions in the Graeco-Roman World, vol. 135. Leiden: Brill.

Vella, H. C. R. 1980. "Quintinus (1536) and St. Paul's Shipwreck in Malta." *Melita Historica* 8(1):61–64.

Venuti, R. 1735. Dissertazione sopra Alcune Medaglie Maltesi." *Saggi di Dissertazioni Accademiche, Pubblicamente lette nella Nobile Accademia Etrusca, dell' Antichissima Città di Cortona* (Rome) 1:36–37.

Vermaseren, M. J. 1956 and 1960. *Corpus Inscriptionum et Monumentorum Religionis Mithriacae,* 2 volumes. The Hague (Netherlands): Hagae Comitis, M. Nijhoff.

—, 1963. *Mithras, the Secretive God.* London: Chatto and Windus.

—, 1971. *Mithriaca I: The Mithraeum at S. Maria Capua Vetere.* Études Préliminaires aux Religions Orientales dans L'Empire Roman. Leiden: E. J. Brill.

Vermeseren, M. J. and van Essen, C. 1964. *The Excavations in the Mithraeum of the Church of Santa Prisca in Rome.* Leiden.

Virzì Hägglund, R. 1976–1977. "Ghar Ta' Iburdan un Insediamento Trogloditico in età Tardo-Romana." *Kokalos* (Istituto di Storia Antica dell'Università di Palermo) 22–23:396–399.

Wasson, R. G. 1968. *Soma, the Divine Mushroom of Immortality,* Ethnomycological Studies, no. 1, new edition 1971. New York: Harcourt Brace Jovanovich.

Wettinger, G. 2000. *Place-Names of the Maltese Islands ca. 1300–1800.* San Gwann (Malta): Publishers Enterprise Group.

Wright, G. R. H.1957. "Cyrene: A Survey of Certain Rock-cut Features to the South of the Sanctuary of Apollo." *The Journal of Hellenic Studies* 77(2):300–310. With an appendix by R. D. Barnett, p. 303.

Zammit, T. 1905–1907. *Archaeological Field-Notes (Note Book No. 1).* Hand written field notes held in the National Museum of Archaeology, Valletta.

—, 1934. "A Decorative Marble Slab Discovered Lately at Notabile – Malta." *Bulletin of the Museum* (Valletta) 1(4):156–157.

INDEX

ILLUSTRATIONS

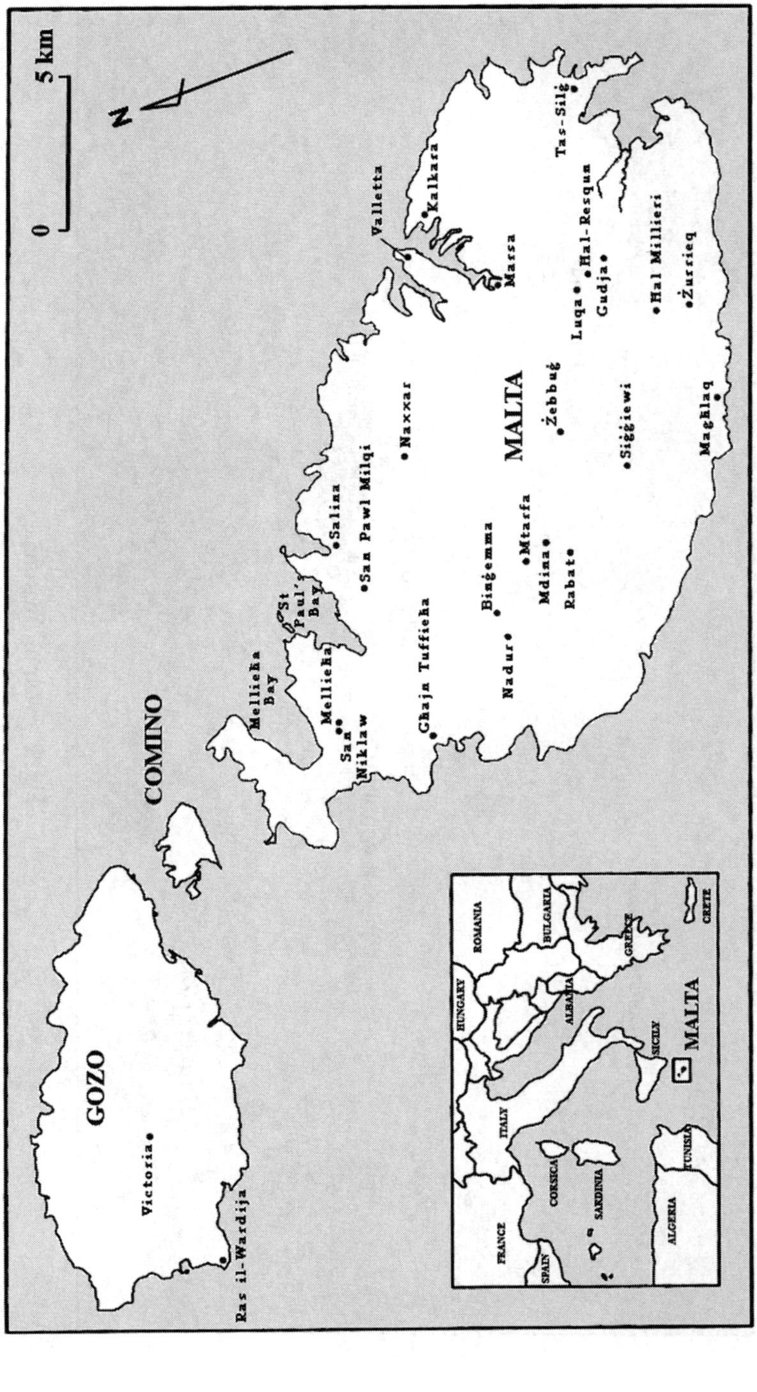

Fig. 1. Map of the Maltese Archipelago.

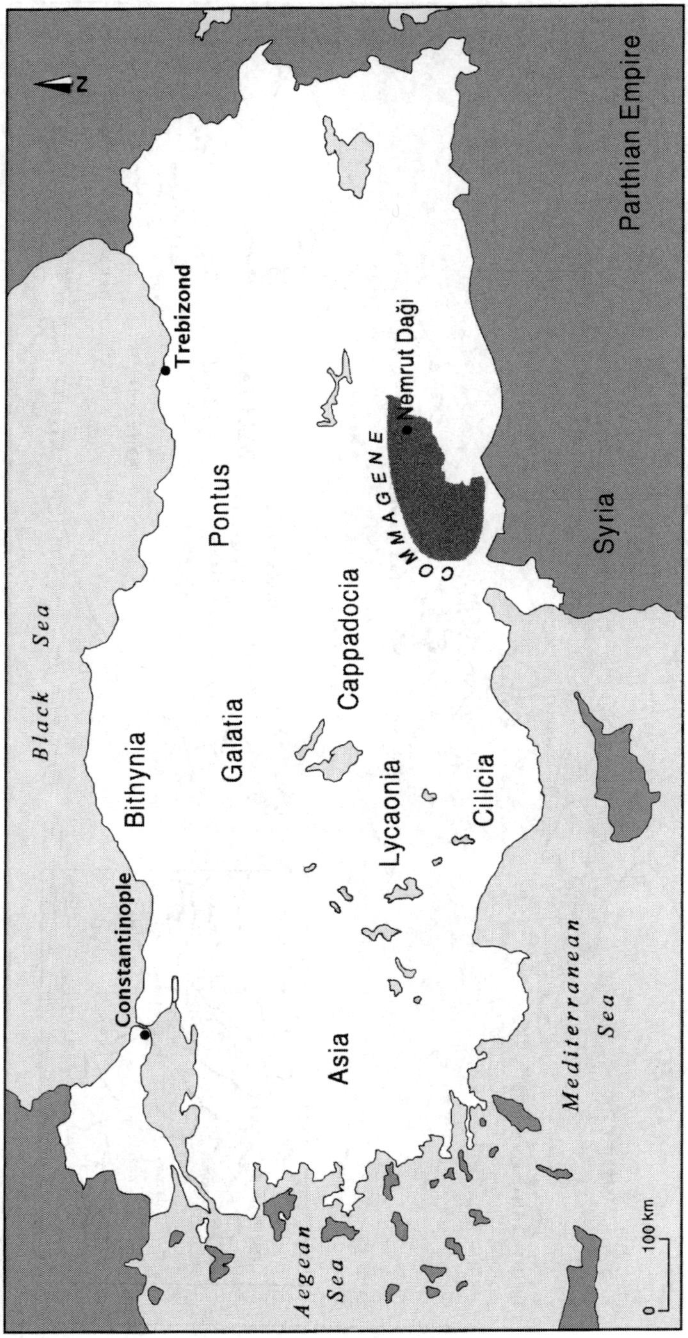

Fig. 2. Map of Anatolia.

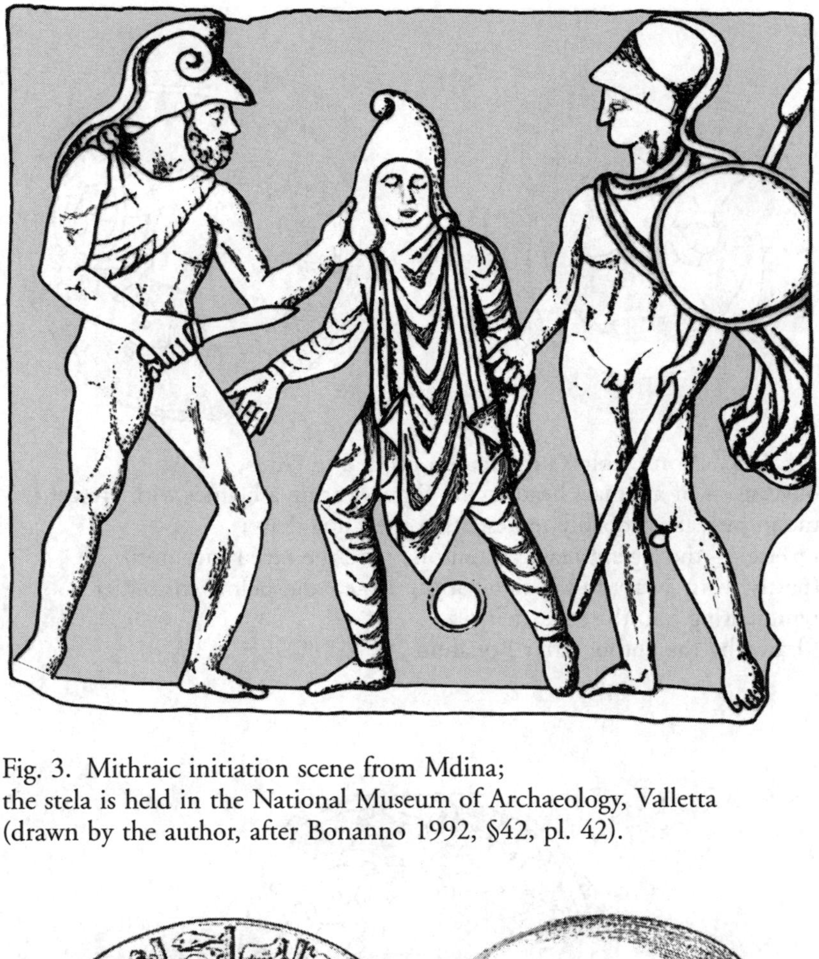

Fig. 3. Mithraic initiation scene from Mdina;
the stela is held in the National Museum of Archaeology, Valletta
(drawn by the author, after Bonanno 1992, §42, pl. 42).

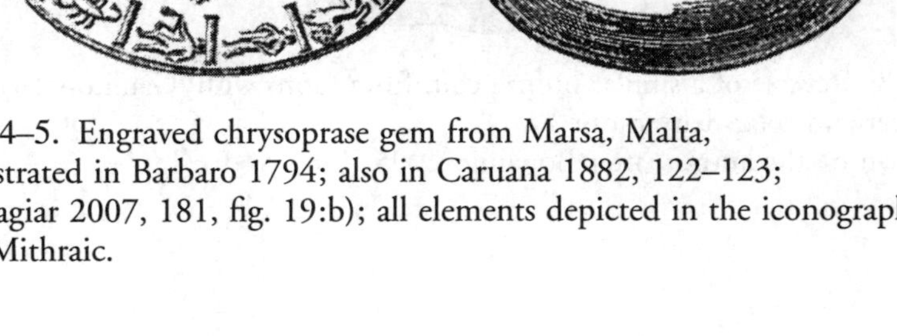

Fig. 4–5. Engraved chrysoprase gem from Marsa, Malta,
(illustrated in Barbaro 1794; also in Caruana 1882, 122–123;
Buhagiar 2007, 181, fig. 19:b); all elements depicted in the iconography
are Mithraic.

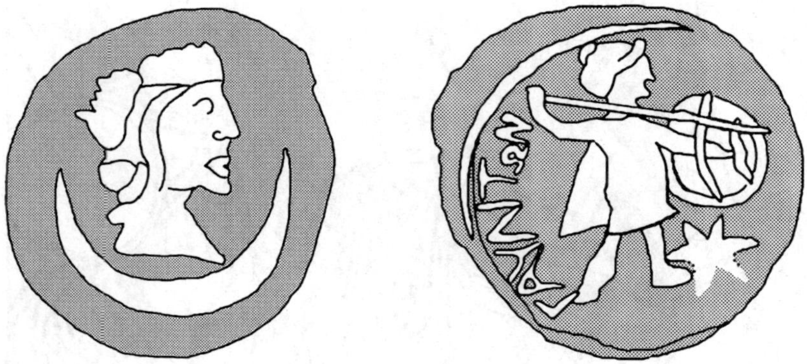

Fig. 6–7. Bronze coin (a quincunx) minted in Gozo;
obverse — of a female head facing right wearing a helmet with crescent moon beneath probably representing the Luna deity;
reverse — the legend reads 'Gauliton', note the rayed sun motif (partly worn away) to the right of the armed and helmeted soldier representing Sol, the solar deity
(drawn by the author, after Bonanno 2005, 159).

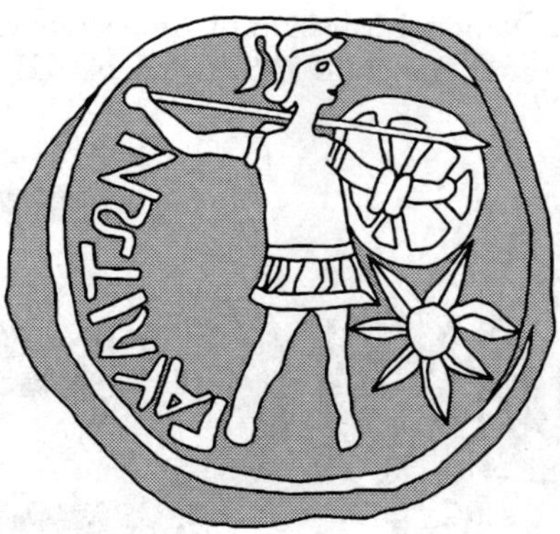

Fig. 8. Reverse of a similar bronze coin from Gozo with 'Gauliton' legend, soldier and solar deity motif
(drawn by the author, after Bonanno 2005, 184).

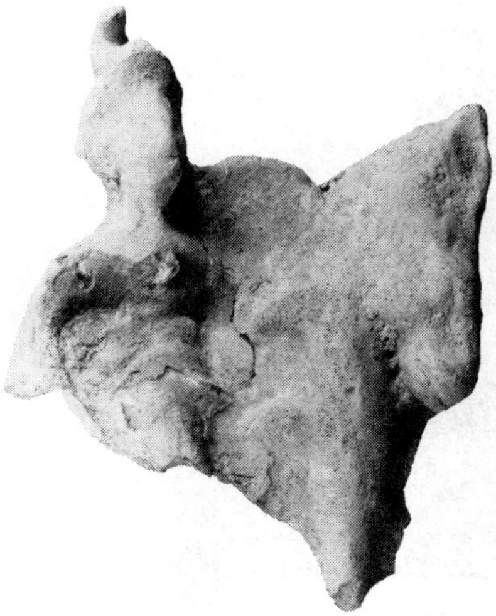

Fig. 9. Terracotta figurine of Mithra on horseback; hollow-made; found in 1951 in Ferris Street, Rabat [596], Tomb 23, contents of shaft (SPA 1995-6; Sagona 2002, 1074, §2, fig. 216:1).

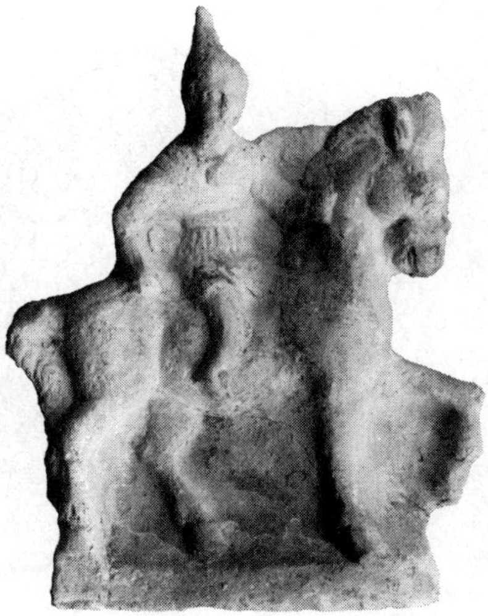

Fig. 10. Terracotta figurine of Mithra on horseback; hollow-made; found in 1951 in Ferris Street, Rabat [596], Tomb 23, contents of shaft (SPA 1995-6; Sagona 2002, 1074, §1, fig. 215:1).

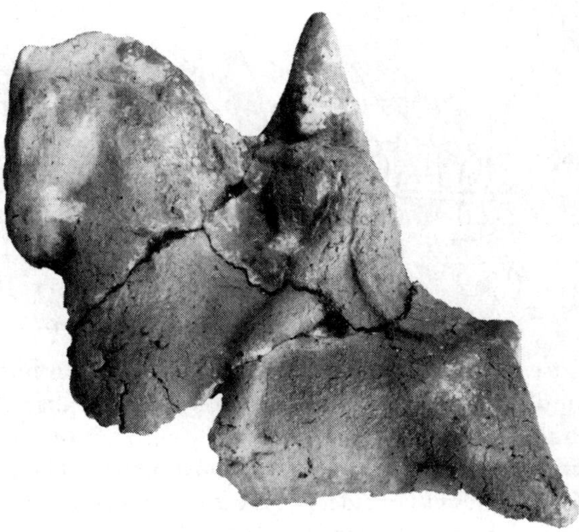

Fig. 11. Terracotta figurine of Mithra on horseback; hollow-made; found in 1951 in Ferris Street, Rabat [596] Tomb 23, contents of shaft (Sagona 2002, 1074, §3, fig. 217:2).

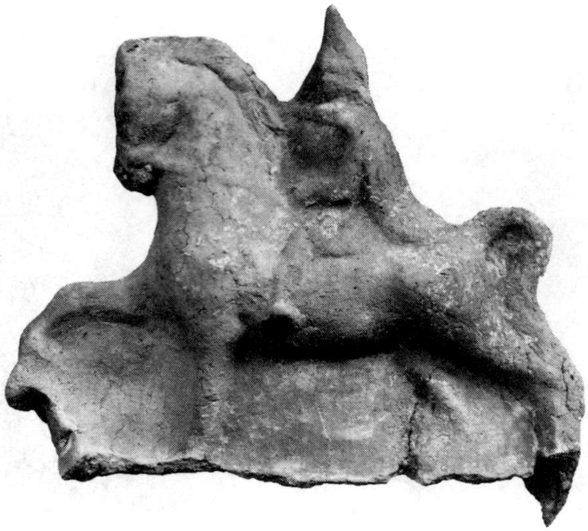

Fig. 12. Terracotta figurine of Mithra on horseback; hollow-made; found in Ferris, Rabat [584], Tomb 11, in Chamber A (Sagona 2002, 1064, §11, fig. 203:1).

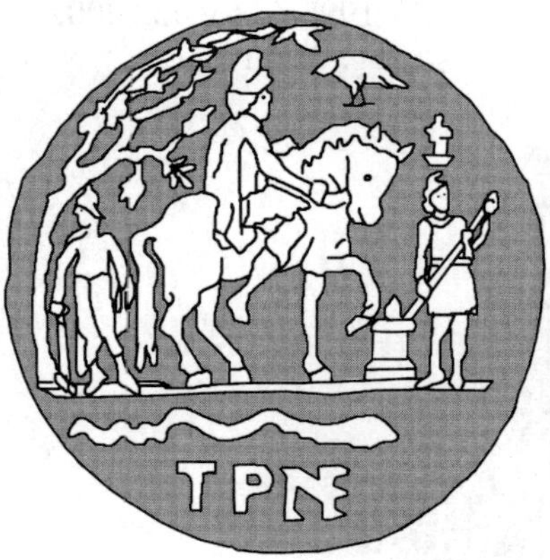

Fig. 13. Reverse face of a bronze coin from Pontic Trabzon (northern Turkey); Mithra on horseback with the torchbearers, Cautes and Cautopates either side. A tree arches over the rider's head. A fire altar is before the horse. On the obverse (not illustrated) is the head of Alexander Severus. The coin is dated to 218 AD (after Cumont 1956, 18, fig. 2:a).

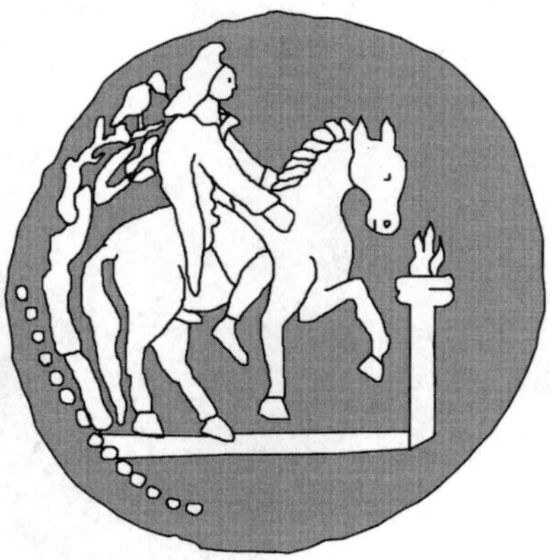

Fig. 14. Mithra on horseback in front of a fire altar. A tree is on the left with a raven sitting on its topmost branch. The obverse of the coin (not illustrated) depicts Alexander Severus (after Cumont 1956, 18, fig. 2:c).

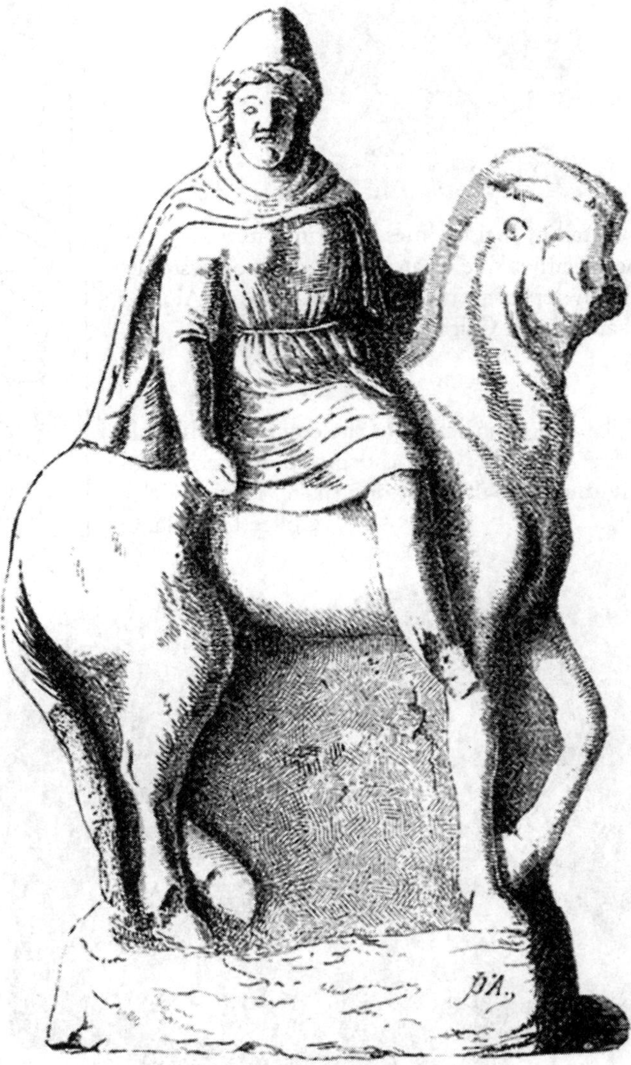

Fig. 15. Figurine of Mithra on horseback
from Carthage
(after Delattre 1898, 9, fig. 15).

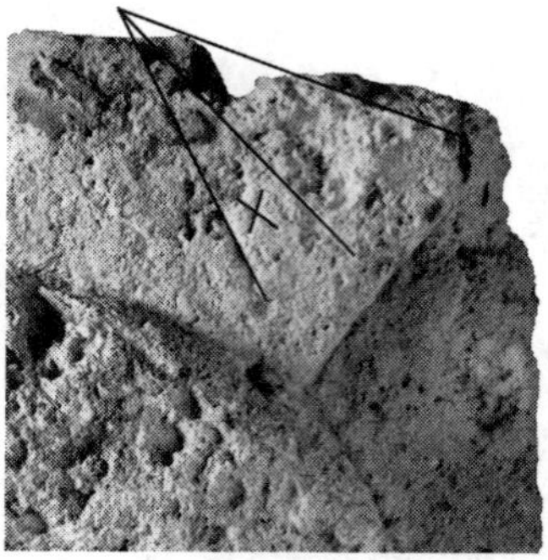

Fig. 16. Detail of incised lines radiating from a central point either side of an incised cross on a stone stela probably representing Mithraic Kronos or Aion, from Rabat. Patrick Galea Collection, Malta.

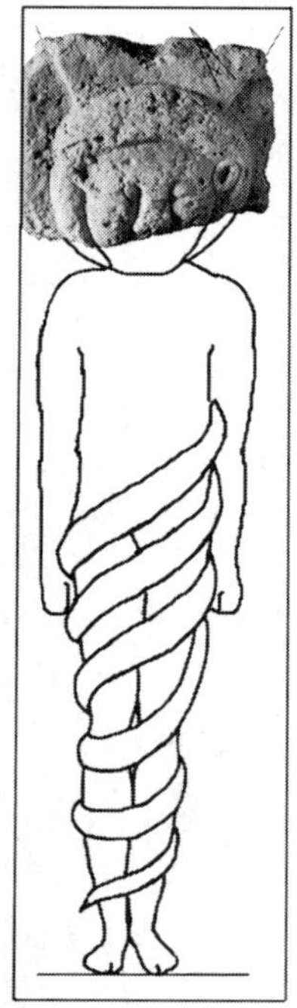

Fig. 17. Likely reconstruction of the complete Mithraic Kronos figure; often this deity is depicted with a human body caught in the coils of a snake. Patrick Galea Collection, Malta.

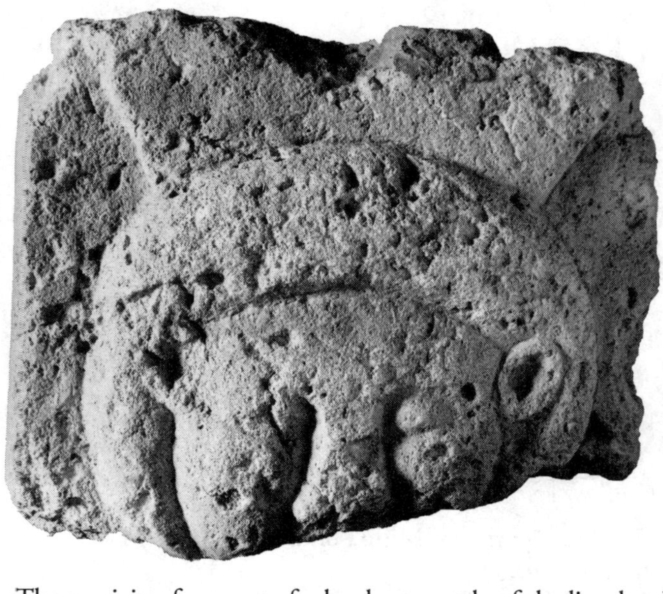

Fig. 18. The surviving fragment of a local stone stela of the lion-headed, Mithraic Kronos or Aion, from Rabat. Note small rounded ears and arch of the main. W 53 cm, H 40 cm, Th 15 cm. Patrick Galea Collection, Malta.

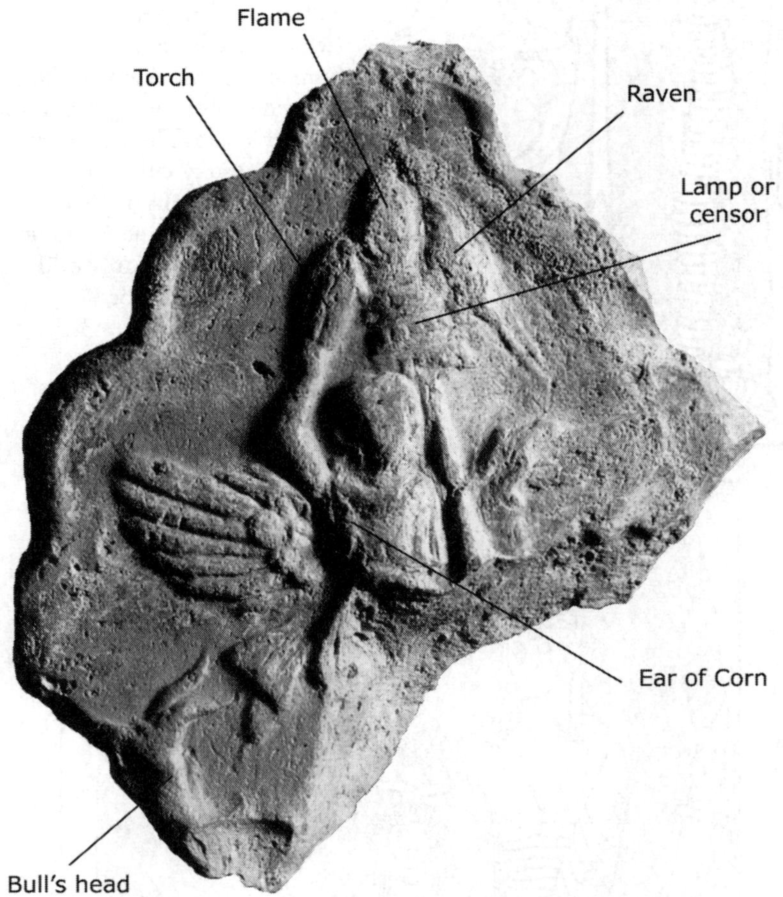

Fig. 19. Terracotta, mould-made plaque with Mithraic figure — perhaps Mithra as Sol Invictus — in the attitude of the torch bearer, Cautes, with torch held above his head. The figure is winged and a bull's head can be seen in the lower left corner. A flaming censor on a staff is behind the figure and a raven is perched on the right side. Saint Agatha's Museum, inv. no. S 12 (SPA 1995/6, 2:23).

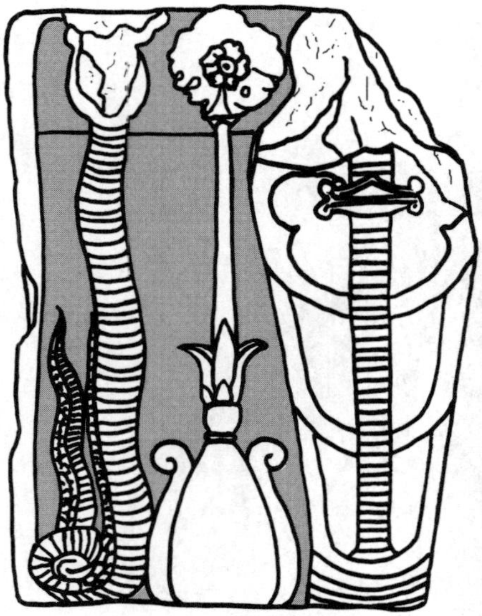

Fig. 20. Carved stela fragment from Malta, possibly from Tas-Silġ; now in a private collection. The serpents (which may have been human-headed) represent Isis, the wide cobra, and Serapis, the thinner snake. The iconography of this mystery cult centred around these consorts has been linked to some Mithraic centres in the Roman world (drawn by the author, after Bonanno 1996, 43).

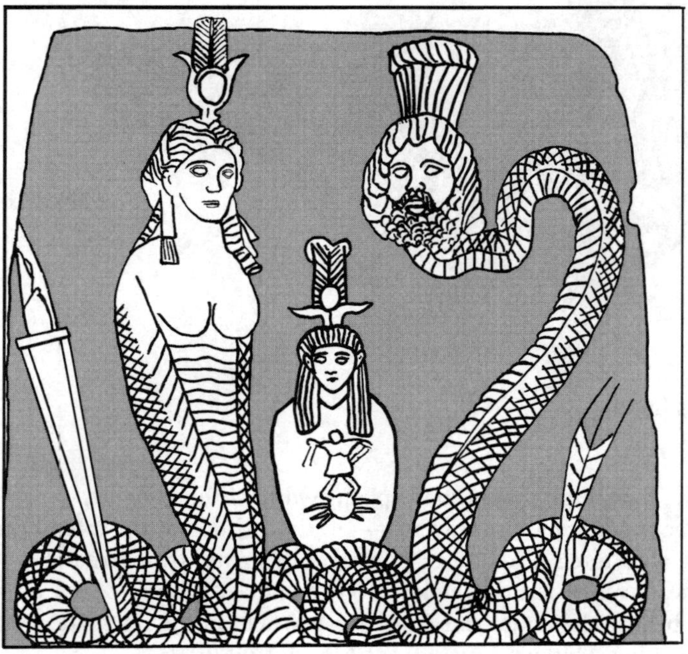

Fig. 21. Stela from El Bahnasa (Egypt) depicting Serapis-headed snake (right) and Isis-headed cobra (left); between them Osiris. This carved stone is held in Rijksmuseum Van Oudheden (drawn by the author, after Bonanno 1996, 45).

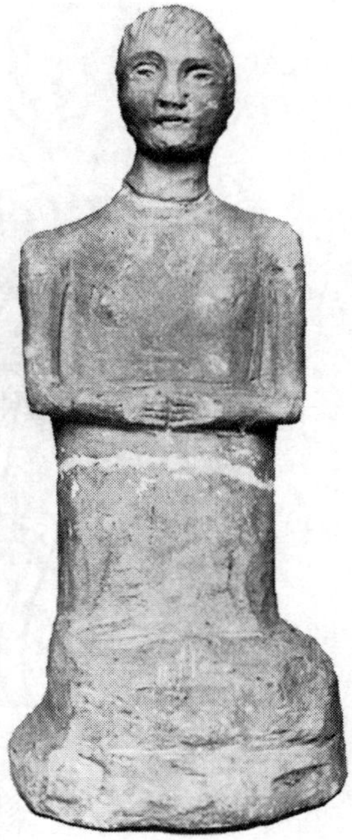

Fig. 22. Figure emerging from a stone, representing the so-called rock-birth of Mithra; carved from local stone. Saint Agatha's Museum inv. no. S 2 (SPA 1995/6, Malta 40:22, 24).

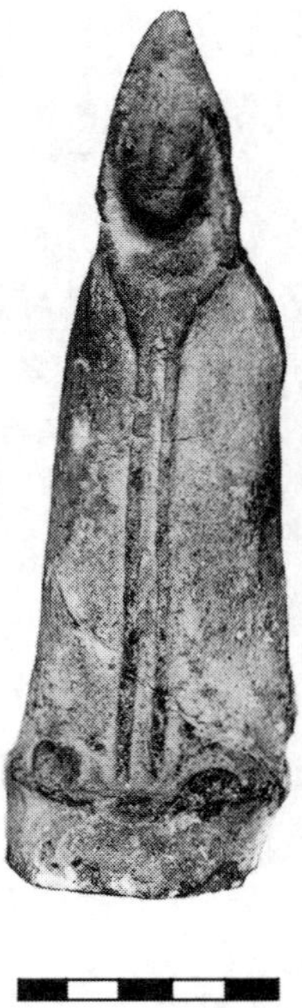

Fig. 23. A standing caped, Mithraic figure with peaked hood; terracotta, mould-made. The feet are sticking out from under the cape. Saint Agatha's Museum, inventory number S 65. (SPA Malta 1995/6, 40:15–16; Sagona 2003, item 572, fig. 53:2).

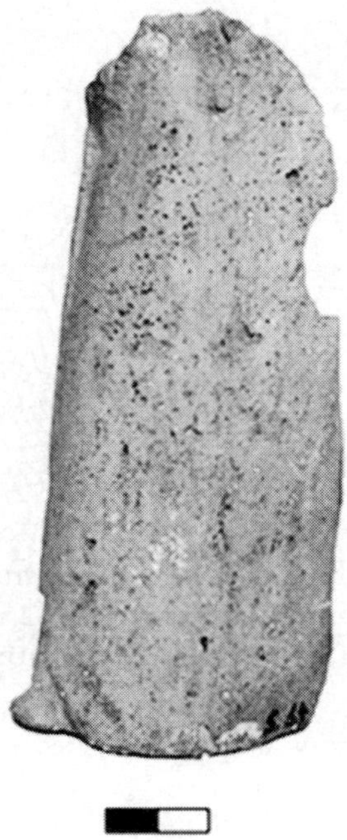

Fig. 24. A caped, Mithraic figurine; terracotta, mould-made; Saint Agatha's Museum, inventory number S 64; damaged (SPA Malta 1995/6, 40:17).

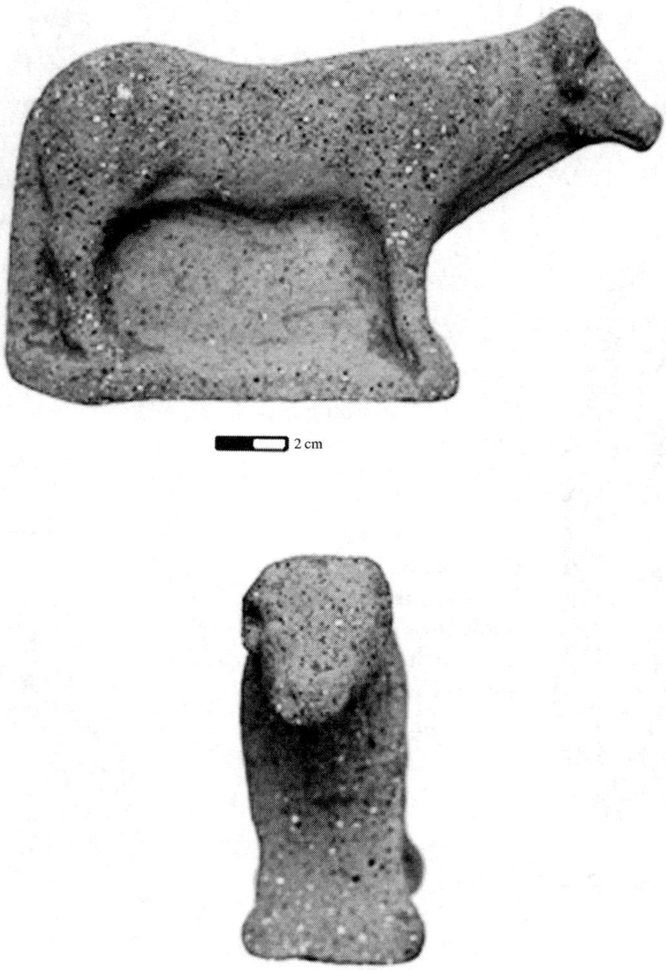

Fig. 25. Bull figurine from Saint Agatha's Museum,
inventory number S 62
(SPA 1995/6, Malta, 40:18–19; Sagona 2003, item 571, fig. 53:3).

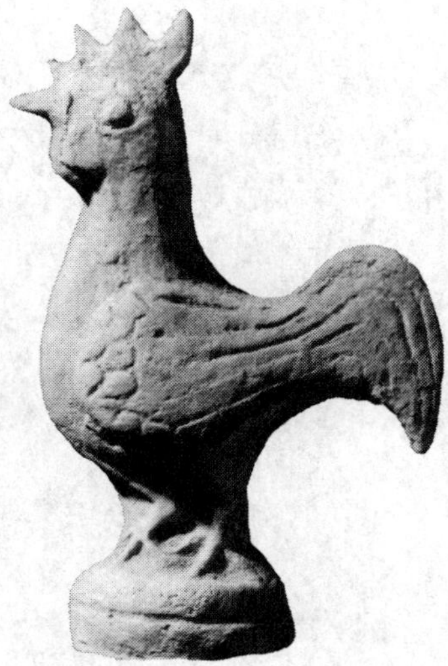

Fig. 26. Cockerel figurine, hollow, mould-made, terracotta from Tomb 4 in New Street, Rabat [421], found in the shaft (Sagona 2002, 971–975, §6, figs 139:26, 140:2; held in the National Museum of Archaeology, Valletta).

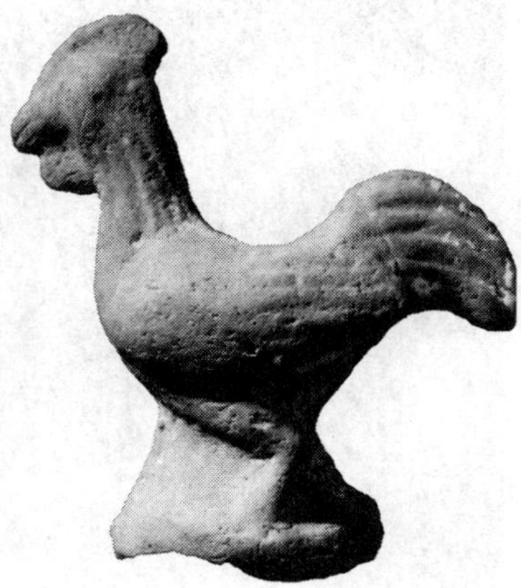

Fig. 27. Cockerel figurine, hollow, mould-made, terracotta unknown provenance, probably from one of the Rabat tombs in New Street (Sagona 2002, fig. 140:3; held in the National Museum of Archaeology, Valletta).

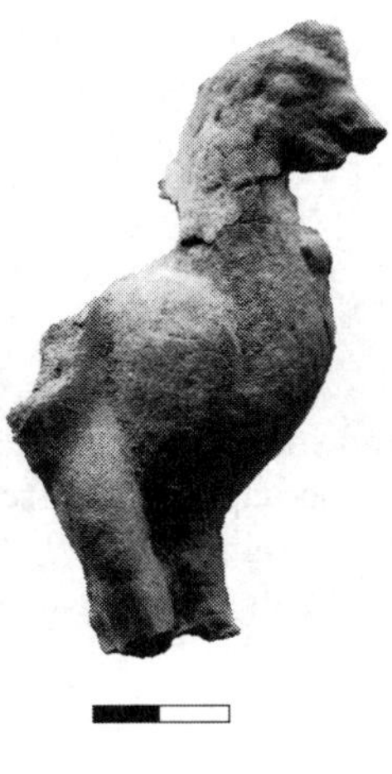

Fig. 28. Cockerel figurine, hollow, mould-made, terracotta from Tomb 23, Ferris Street, Rabat [596], from the shaft (SPA 1995-6; Sagona 2002, 1074–1075, §4 figs 216:2, 217:4; held in the National Museum of Archaeology, Valletta).

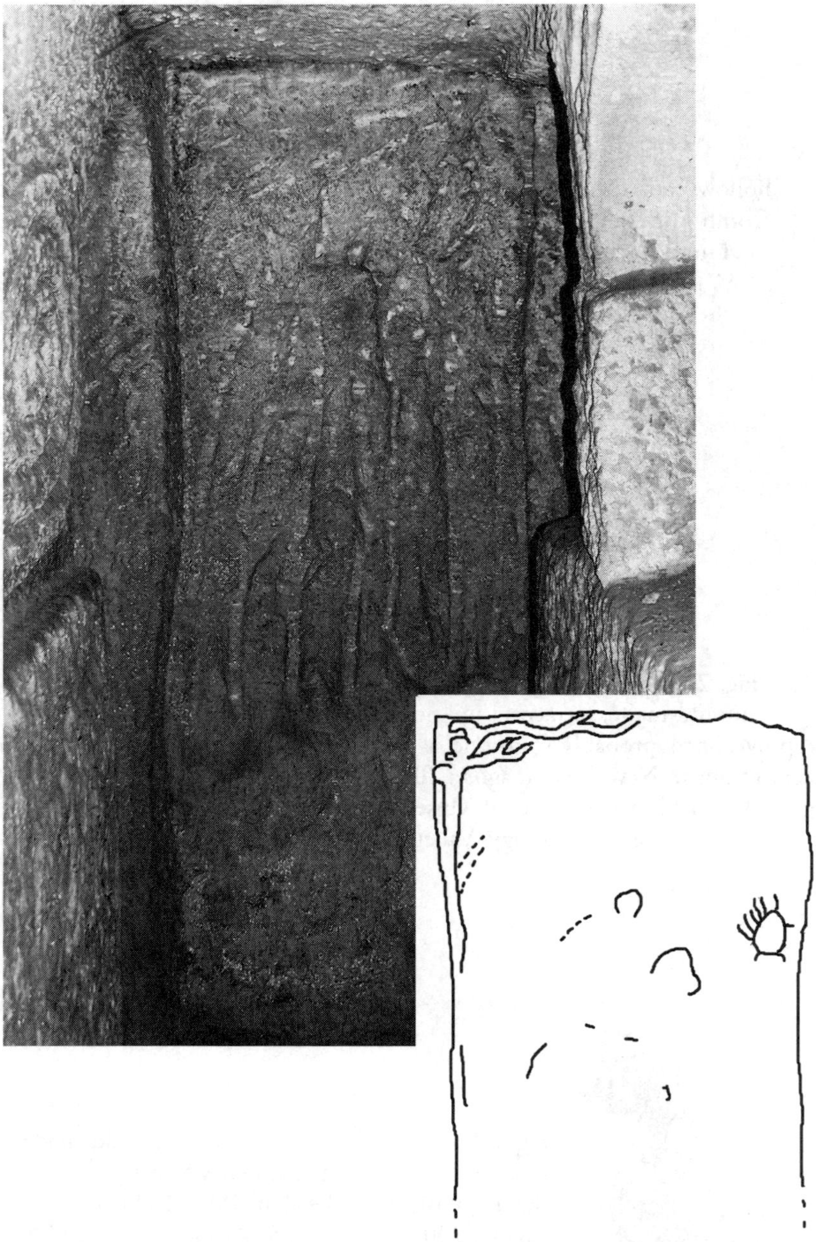

Fig. 29. Carved wall (deliberately defaced in antiquity) in a catacomb in Salina, northern Malta, which might represent Mithra perhaps on a horse. A circular shape with rays around it appears to be on the right side of the central figure possibly a depiction of Sol or a flaming altar (photo supplied by Keith Buhagiar).

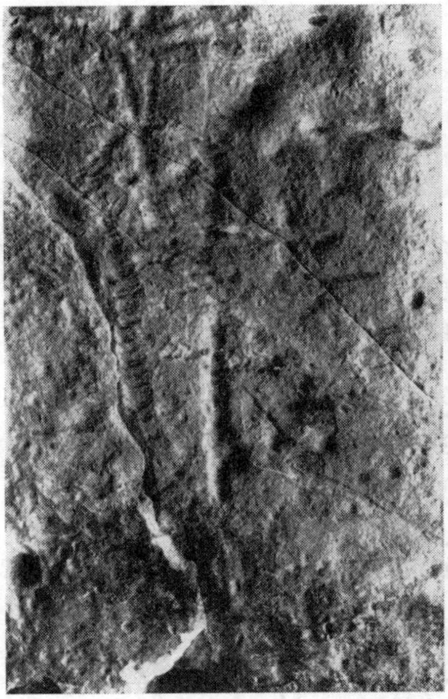

Fig. 30. Carving in the north wall of the cave at Ras il-Wardija, at point 15 in Fig. 55 (after *Missione Archeologica Italiana a Malta*, 1966, [for 1965], fig. 83:2, courtesy of Professor M. P. Rossignani).

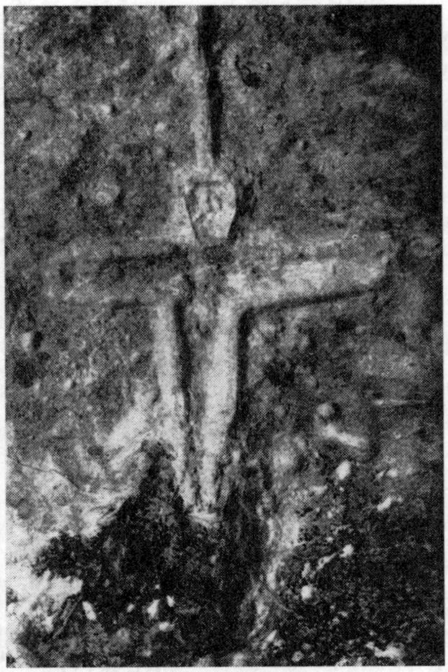

Fig. 31. Carving in the niche cut in the south wall of the cave at Ras il-Wardija, at point 5 in Fig. 55 (after *Missione Archeologica Italiana a Malta*, 1966, [for 1965], fig. 83:3, courtesy of Professor M. P. Rossignani).

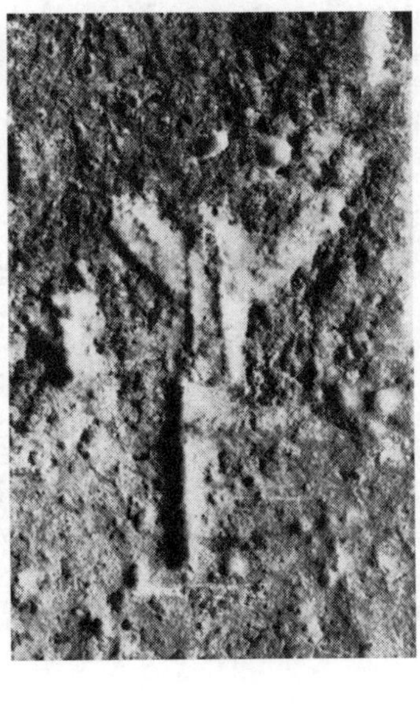

Fig. 32. Carving in the south wall of the cave at Ras il-Wardija, at point 16 in Fig. 55 (after *Missione Archeologica Italiana a Malta*, 1966, [for 1965], fig. 83:1, courtesy of Professor M. P. Rossignani).

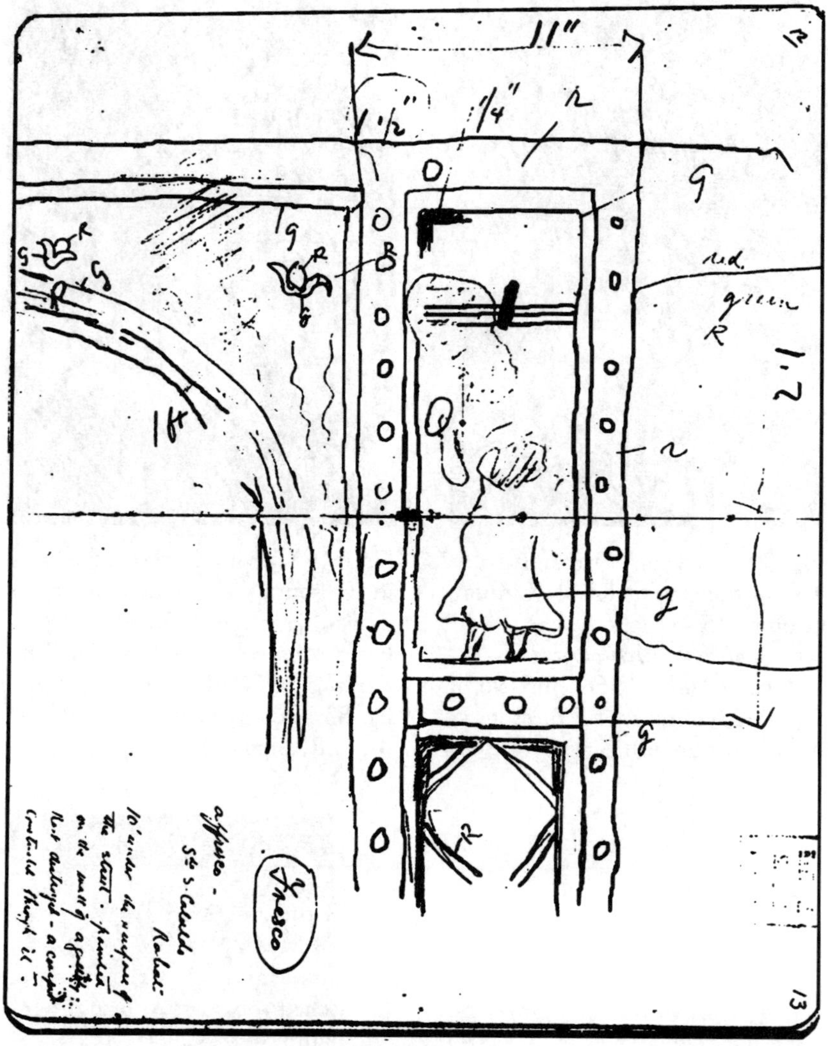

Fig. 33. Page from T. Zammit's field notebook for 1905–1907 (Notebook I), 12–13; held in the archive of the National Museum of Archaeology, Malta. He sketched the fresco painted on a gallery wall in 'Strada S. Cataldo, Rabat'. The fresco was executed in red and green paint. Of the site Zammit's writes, "10' under the surface of the street. Painted on the wall of a gallery. Most destroyed — a cesspit constructed through it."

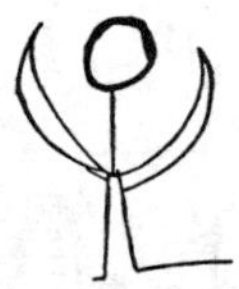

Fig. 34. A Mithraic symbol painted on a sherd from Dura Europos (Syria), Room H, M7 (after Vermaseren 1960, vol. 2, 14, fig. 243).

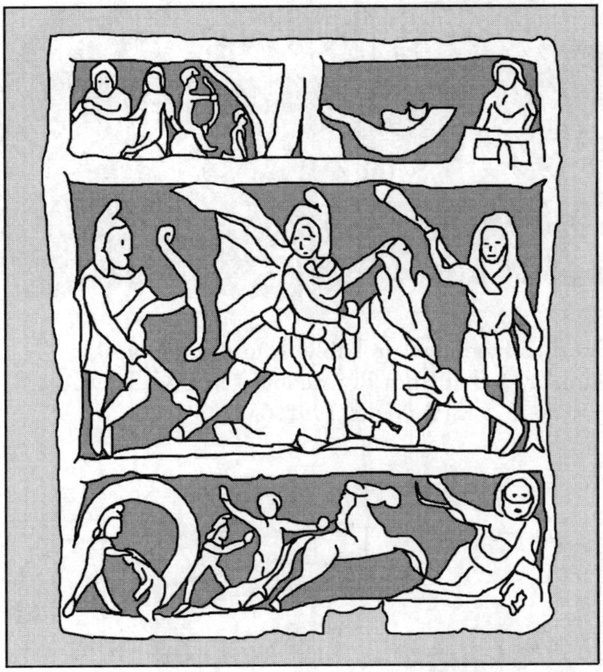

Fig. 35. Relief from Roustchouk (Ruse), near the junction of the Danube and Lom Rivers; held in the National Museum of Sofia.
Top left panel (left to right): bust of Sol; Mithra leaning on a rock with his left arm; Mithra firing his arrow at the arched rock face to bring forth life giving water; a kneeling Mithraic figure.
Top right panel: a bull in a boat and bust of Luna behind a balustrade.
Middle panel: Cautopates with torch lowered in his right hand and bow in his left; Mithra slaughtering the bull, a dog jumps up to lick its blood; Cautes with torch held up in his right hand and *pedum* (shepherd's crook) in his left hand.
Lower panel: Mithra puts his hand on Sol's head in cave setting; Mithra ascends in the Sun's chariot; the bearded god Oceanus leans on his left arm and waves his right arm to Sol in a greeting
(after Vermaseren 1960, vol. 2, mon. 2272, 357, fig. 632).

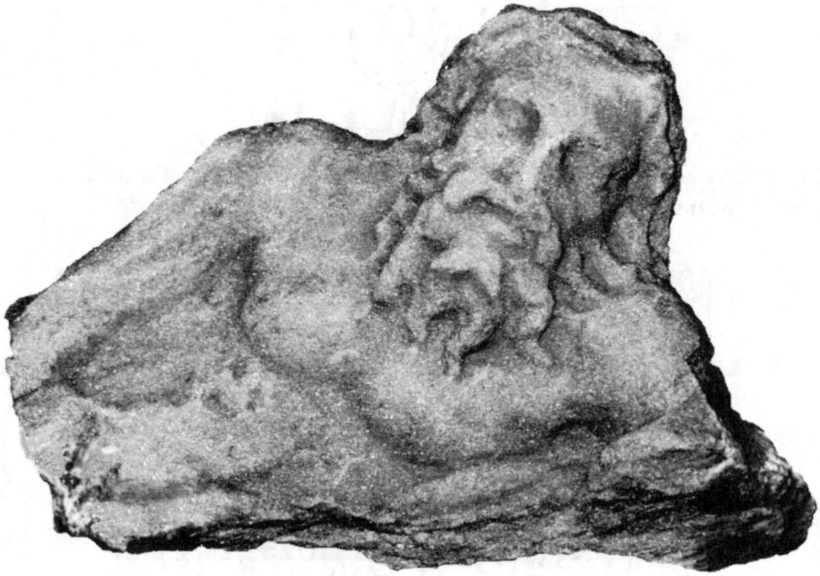

Fig. 36. Oceanus fragment, probably from a larger work (probably similar to that from Roustchouk) held in Saint Agatha's Museum inv. no. S 5 (SPA Malta 1995/6, 2:23).

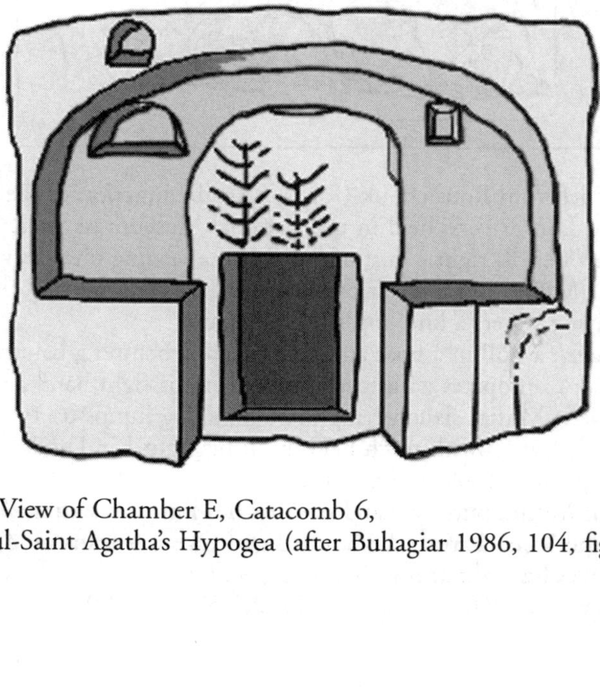

Fig. 37. View of Chamber E, Catacomb 6,
Saint Paul-Saint Agatha's Hypogea (after Buhagiar 1986, 104, fig. 28).

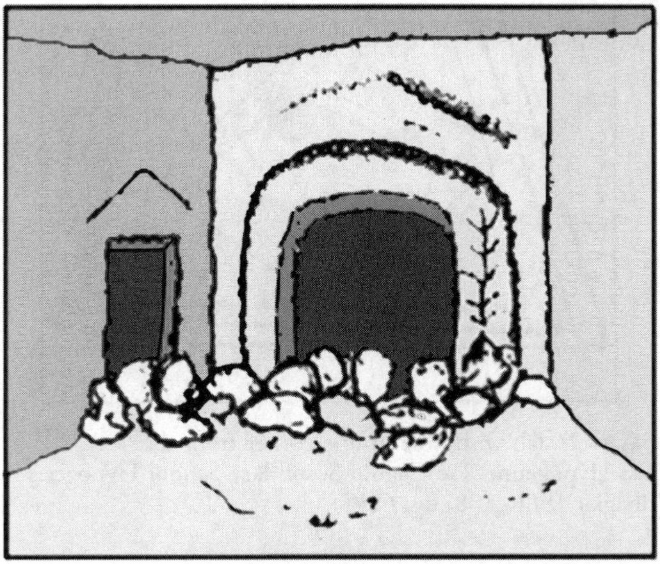

Fig. 38. View of the tomb, Ingieret 1, Luqa (after Buhagiar 1986, 259).

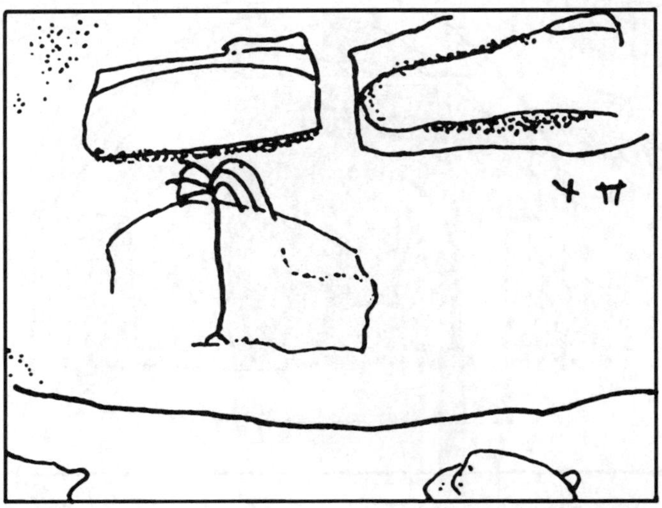

Fig. 39. Palm tree incised on a wall emerging through an arched canopy; from the South-East Hypogeum, Tac-Caghqi Secondary School Hypogea (after Borg and Rocco 1972, 72, fig. 2).

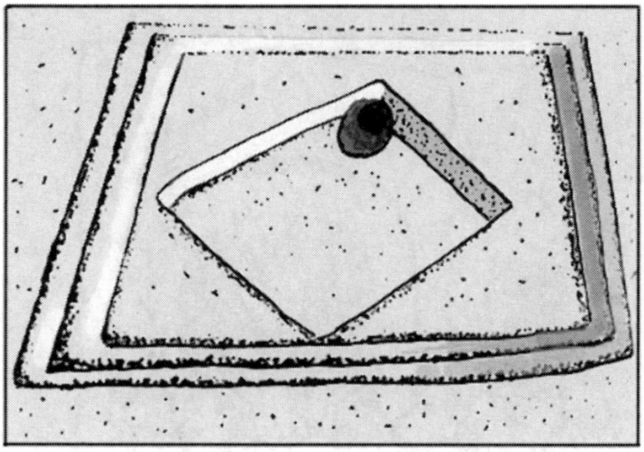

Fig. 40. Carved slab with hole in one corner from the South-East Hypogeum, Tac-Caghqi Secondary School Hypogea (after Buhagiar 1986, 188, fig. 60:C).

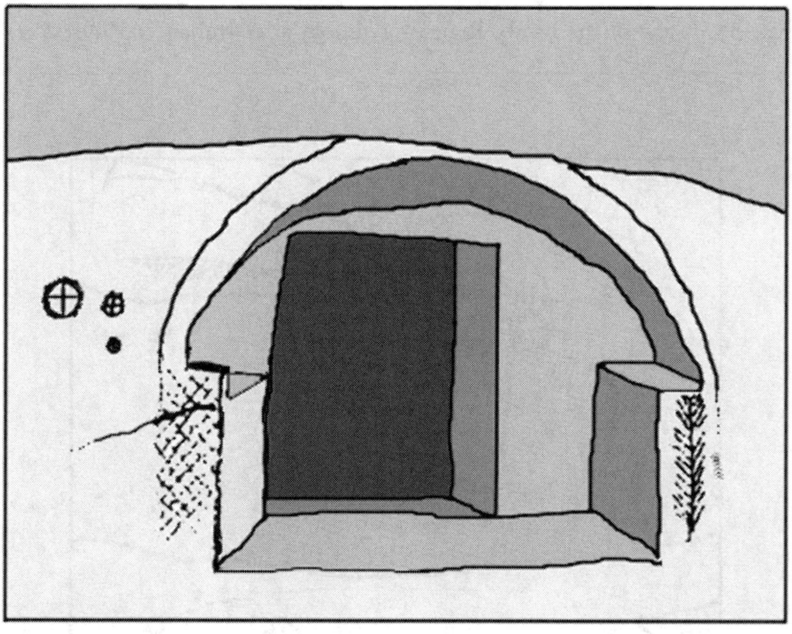

Fig. 41. View of the entrance to Tomb 7, Mqabba, Tal-Kandja Hypogeum showing the incised palm frond on the right side of the entrance. The other side is scored probably to prepare the surface for plaster, now lost. Three small discs with lightly incised stars or crosses are on the left (after Buhagiar 1986, 322, fig. 105:C).

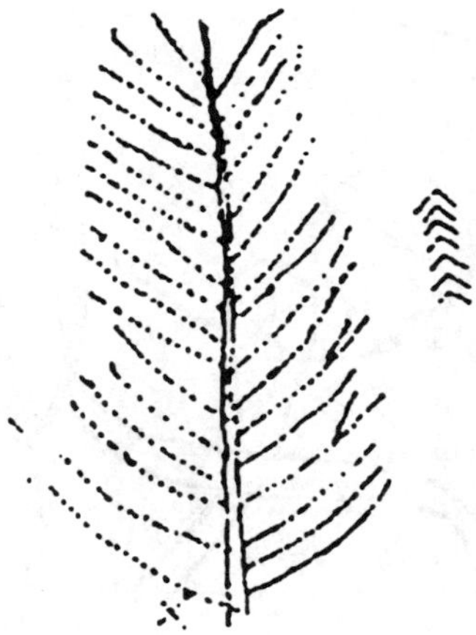

Fig. 42. Detail of the palm from Tomb 7 in the Mqabba, Tal-Kandja Hypogeum.

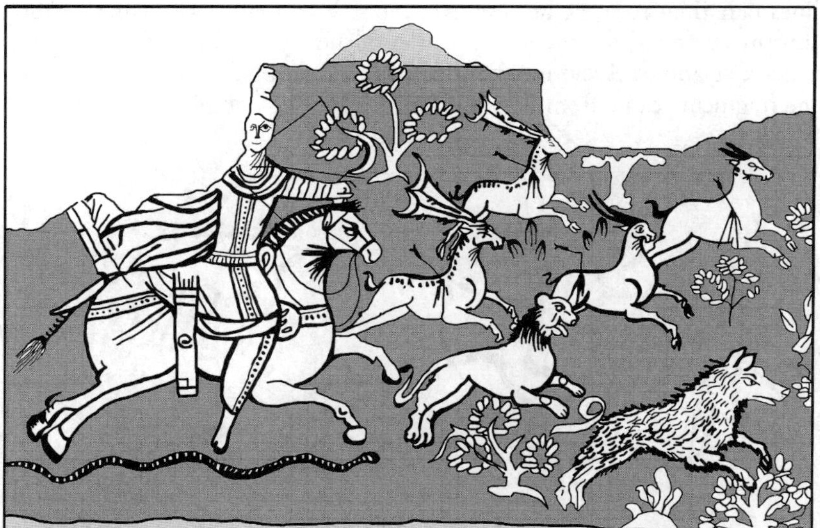

Fig. 43. Fresco from the mithraeum in Dura Europos, Syria, depicting Mithra on horseback hunting with bow and arrow; a snake is beside the horse and wounded, wild animals run before the hunter; dated to 240 AD (after Gates 1984, 166–167).

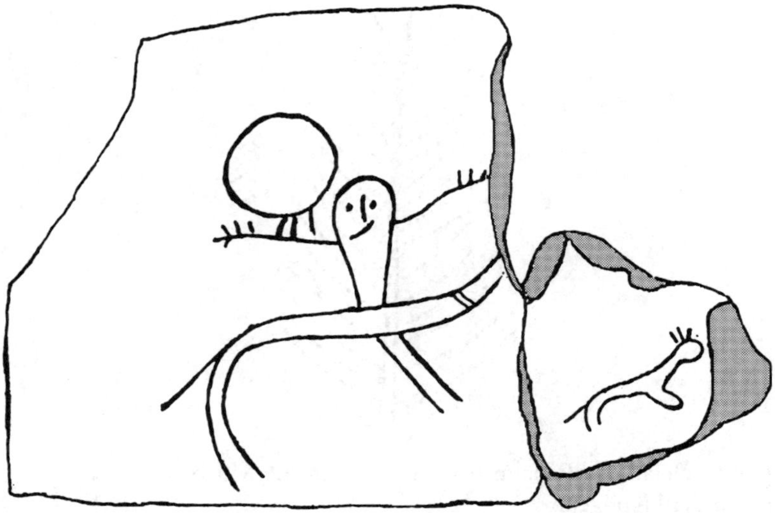

Fig. 44. Graffito probably depicting Mithra on horseback with a quadruped (a dog?) running in front deeply scratched on stone blocks from the religious precinct of Tas-Silġ, southern Malta. The disc with lines radiating from the bottom over the stylised figure may represent the sun thus emphasising the identification of the figure with the solar deity (after Cagiano de Azevedo, *et al.* 1967 [for 1966], pl. 26:1, the fragments came from Room 20 in the Tas-Silġ complex).

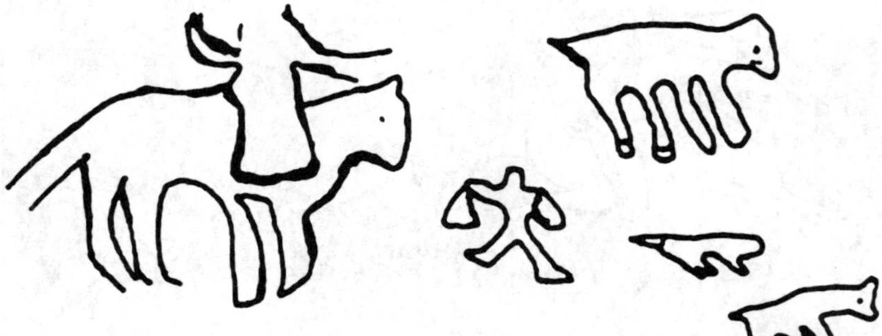

Fig. 45. Graffito scratched in a stone block (now lost) in a house wall in Triq Santa Maria, Gudja. The scene depicts Mithra on horseback, Cautes the torchbearer walks in front and animals flee before them (after Buhagiar 2001, 17, fig. 5:b).

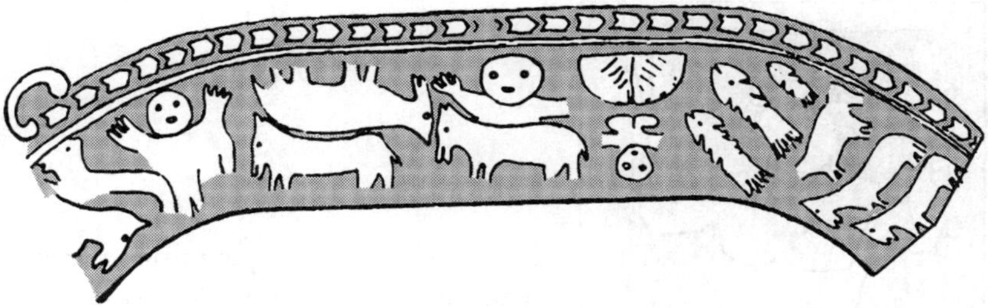

Fig. 46. Figures with arms raised up from Ħal Resqun catacomb, Gudja, representing Mithra as the sun in three positions, dawn, day and sunset (or Mithra and the torch-bearers Cautes and Cautopates in the centre, left and right respectively). Quadrupeds and fish surround the figures (after Buhagiar 1986, 36, fig. 9:a).

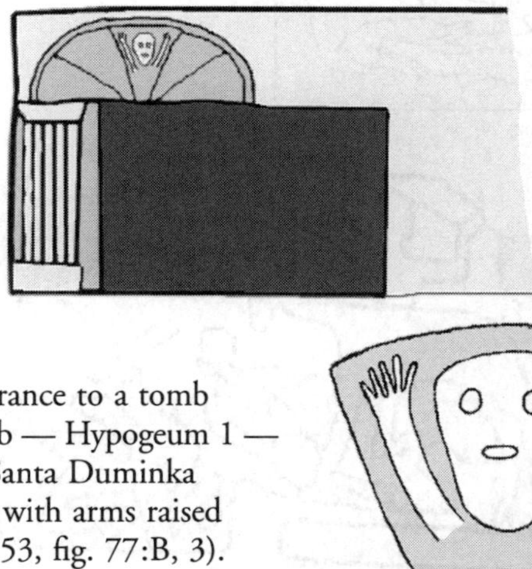

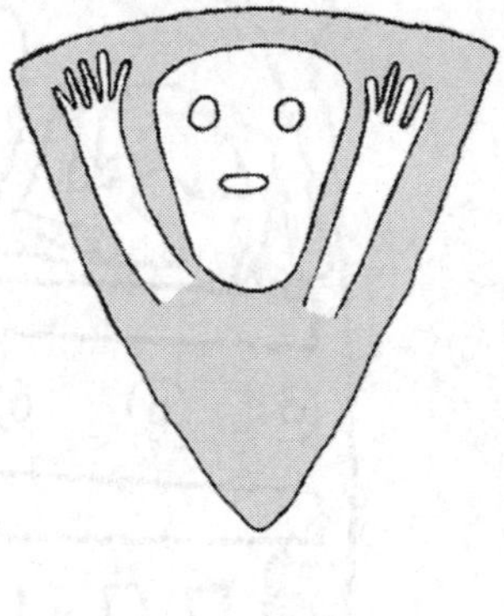

Fig. 47. Decorated entrance to a tomb chamber in the catacomb — Hypogeum 1 — at Kalkara, Xaghra ta' Santa Duminka and detail of the figure with arms raised (after Buhagiar 1986, 253, fig. 77:B, 3).

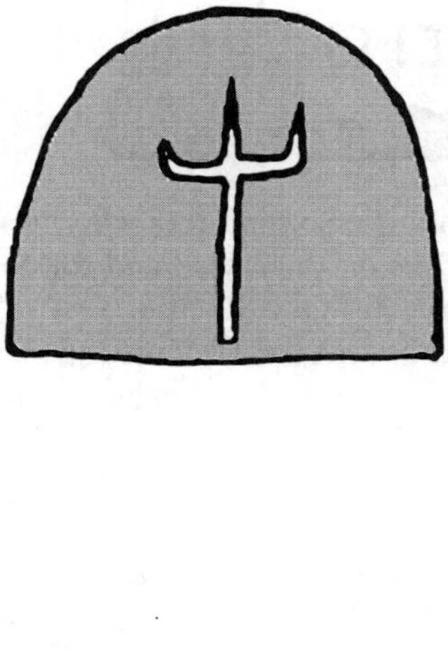

Fig. 48. A niche in Tomb 5 in Xaghra tal-Maghlaq, Qrendi, with Mithraic stylised figure carved in the back wall (after Buhagiar 1986, 330, fig. 108:A, 3, aa).

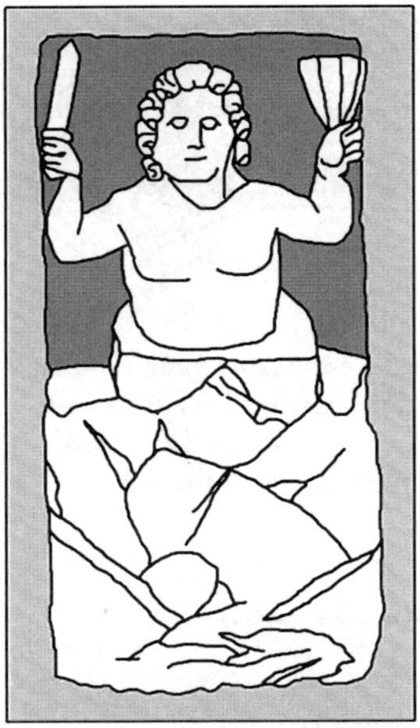

Fig. 49. Mithra emerging from a rock with ears of wheat in his left hand (an unusual depiction) and sword in his right hand; from Cologne (after Clauss 2000, 64, fig. 23).

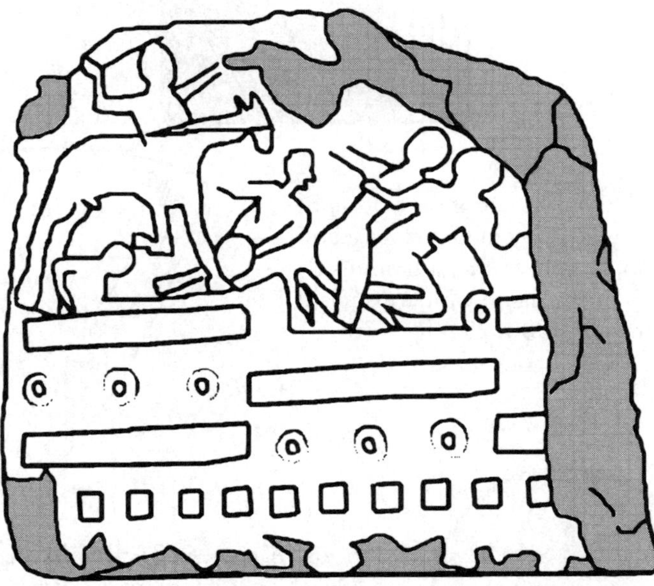

Fig. 50. Carved stone perhaps depicting Mithra overcoming foes who fall in front or under the horse, some have cut marks on their head and torso; the block comes from the grounds of the church at Ħal Millieri (after Buhagiar 1976, fig. 10B). A copy is held in St Agatha's Museum with a second original, joining fragment on the right depicting what appears to be animals fleeing to the right.

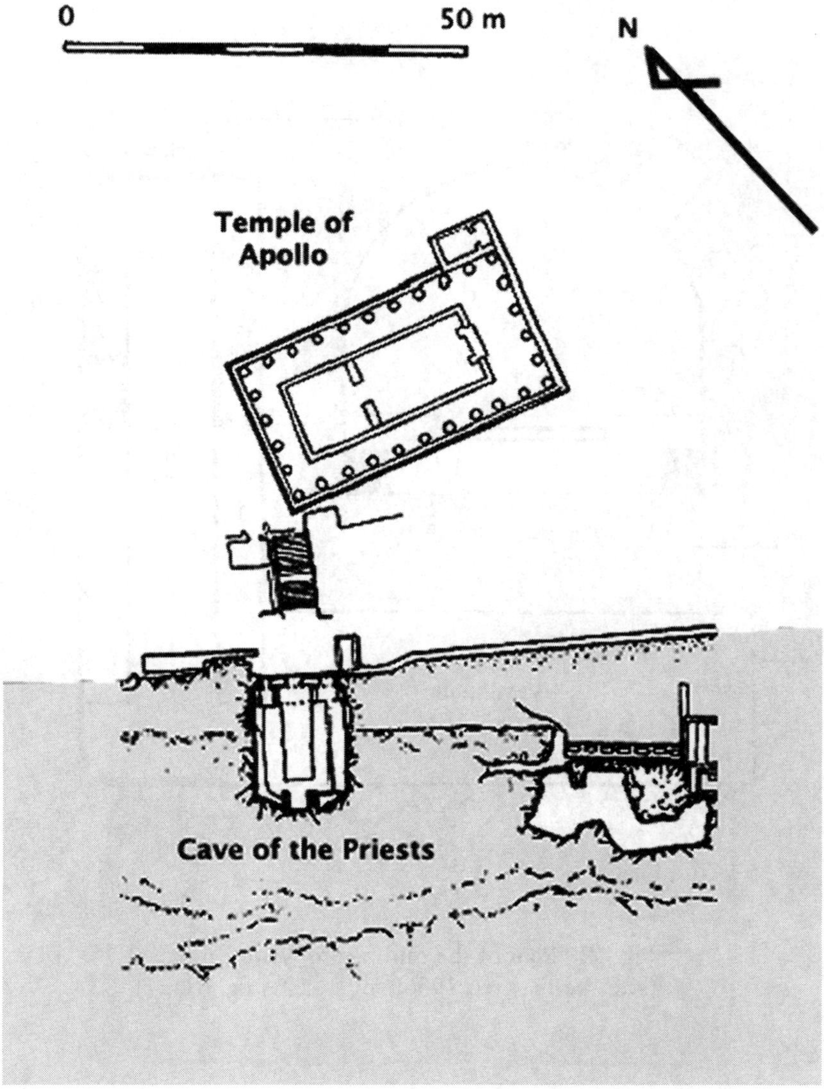

Fig. 51. Plan of the rock-cut mithraeum from Cyrene with temple of Apollo in front, to the east: (after Wright 1957, fig. 1).

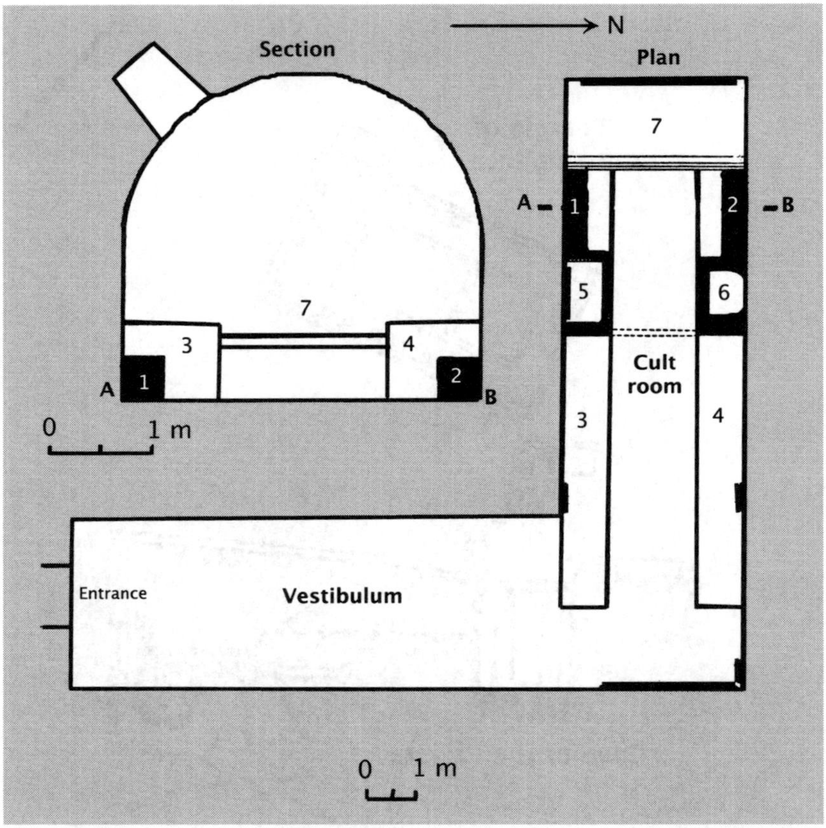

Fig. 52. Plan of the mithraeum from Capua (after Vermaseren 1956, vol. 1, 105, fig. 51).

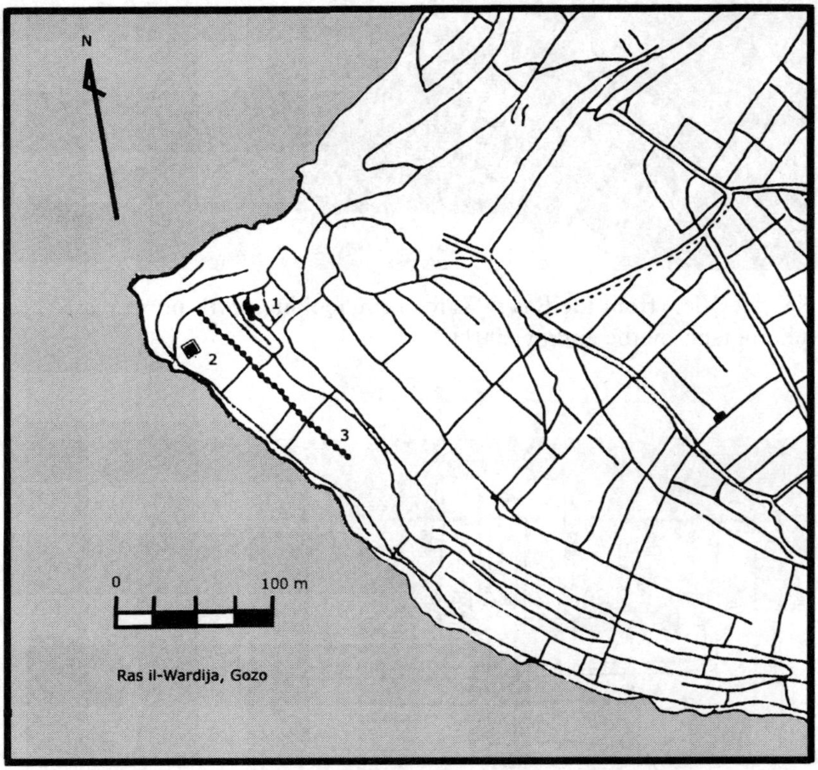

Fig. 53. Map of Ras il-Wardija in Gozo showing the rock-cut cave (1), which is likely to be a mithraeum, the open air temple (2) — a structure built on the site probably in the Punic period — and an early foot path (3) that lead to the site.

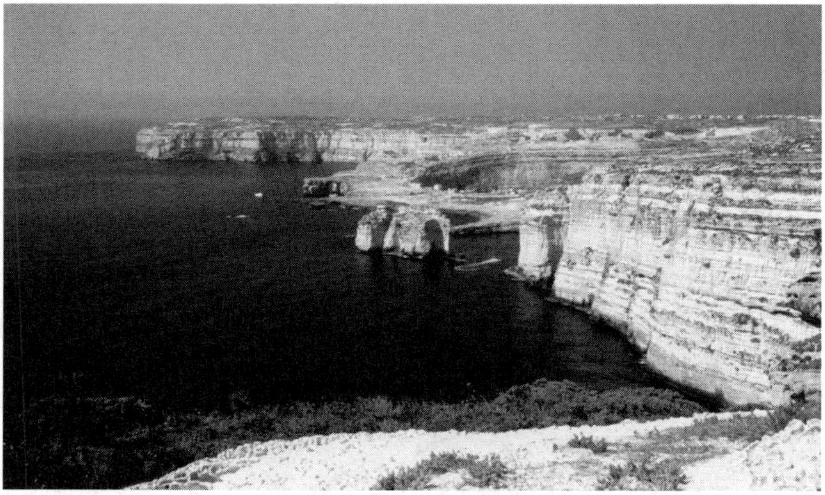

Fig. 54. View from the Ras il-Wardija site looking north north east (photograph by the author 2001).

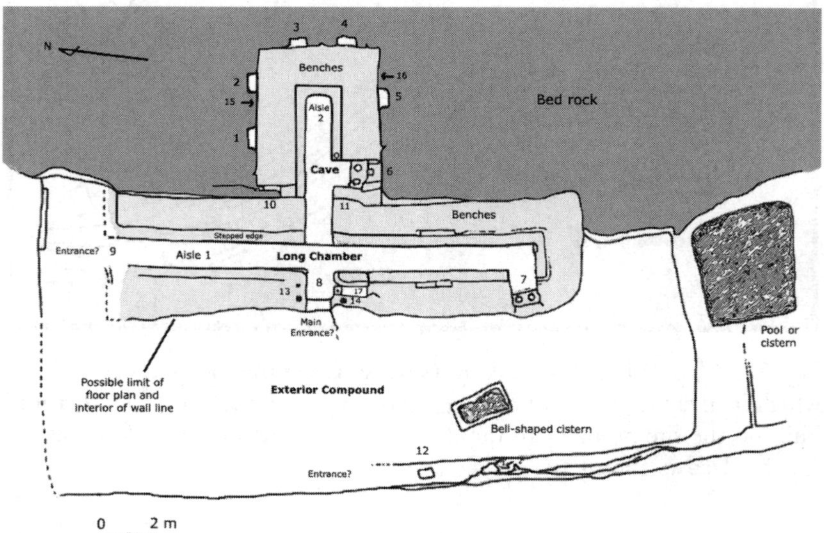

Fig. 55. Plan of the possible mithraeum at Ras il-Wardija, Gozo (after Cagiano de Azevedo, *et al.* 1967). Features include: 1–5 rectangular niches cut into the cave walls, 6–7 altars, 8 the main entrance, 9 possibly a second entrance, 10–11 remains of a partitioning wall, 12 socket for a monument or an upright post, 13–14 door sockets, 15–16 positions of graffiti (another is at point 5), 17 socket for a monument or an upright post.

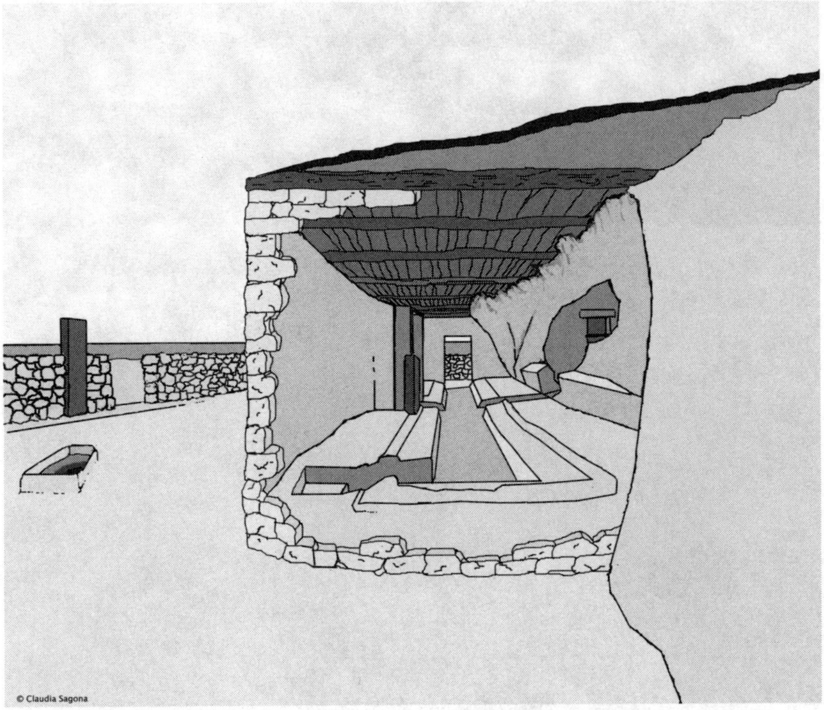

Fig. 56. Impression of the Ras il-Wardija site showing the walls of the building in front of the rock-cut cave, the deep aisles cut into the floor forming benches against the walls and the outer compound wall (drawing by the author based on a photograph in Cagiano de Azevedo *et al.* 1967, taken shortly after excavation).

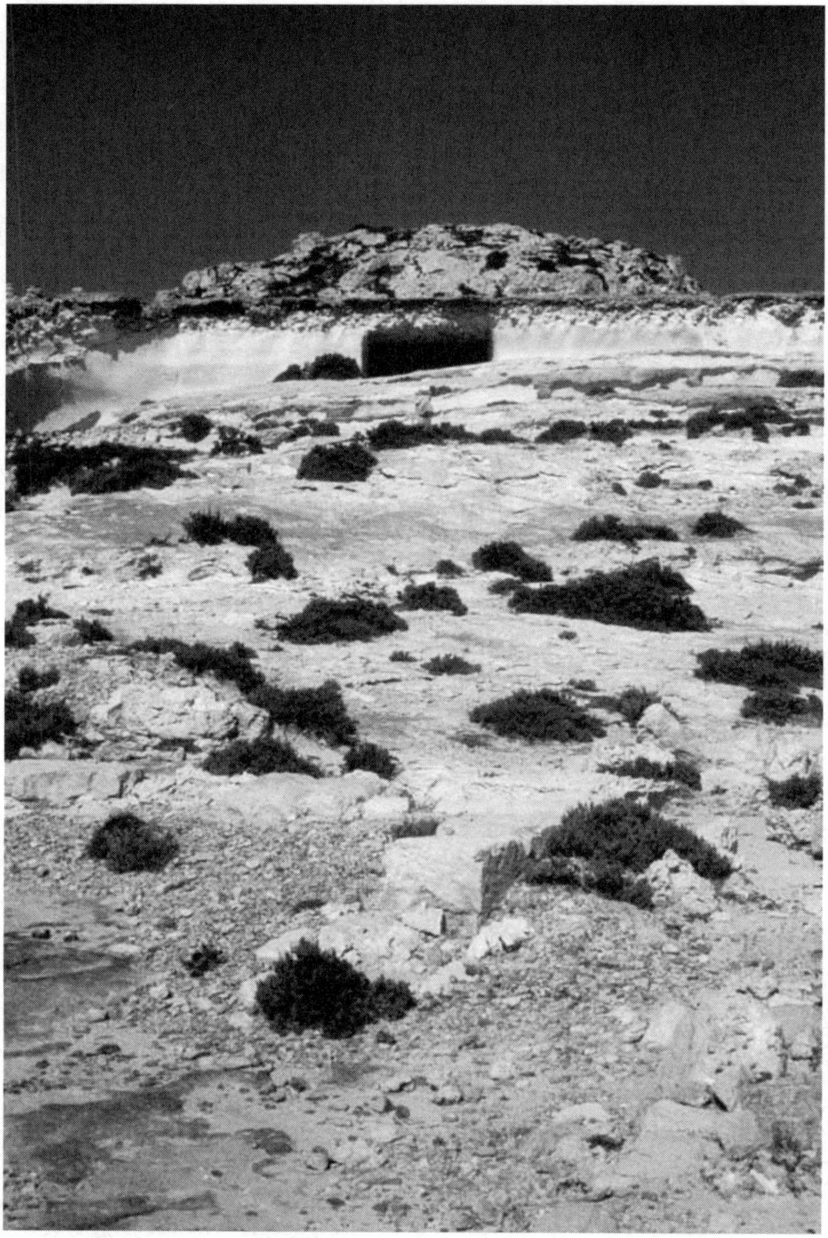

Fig. 57. View of the Ras il-Wardija site looking north east from the foundations of the open air temple in the foreground to the rock-cut cave higher on the slope (photograph by the author 2001).

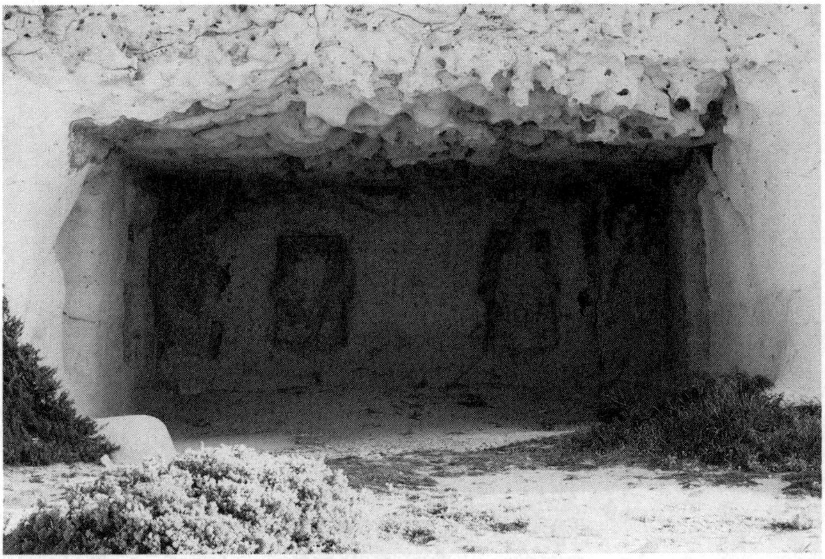

Fig. 58. Ras il-Wardija, the interior rear wall of the rock-cut cave with two of the five rectangular niches (photograph by the author 2001).

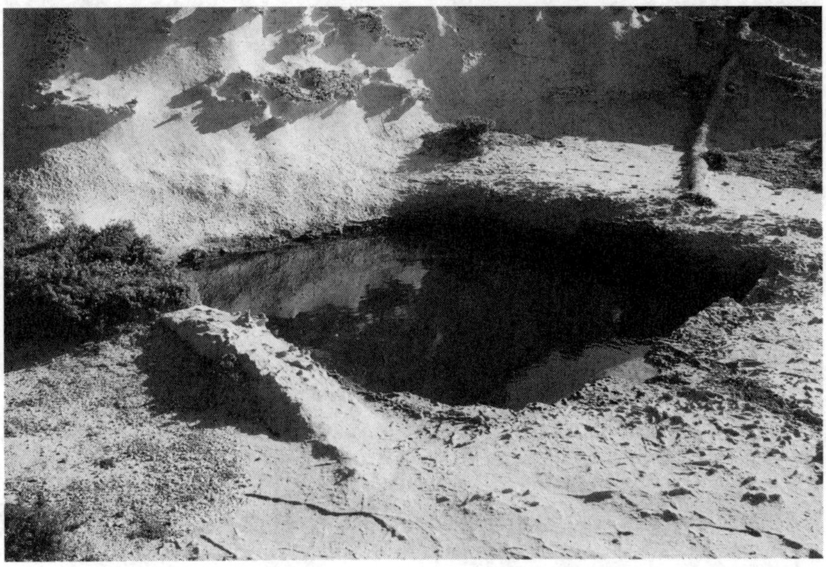

Fig. 59. Ras il-Wardija, the rock cut pool filled with water, there are access steps down one side (photograph by the author 2001).

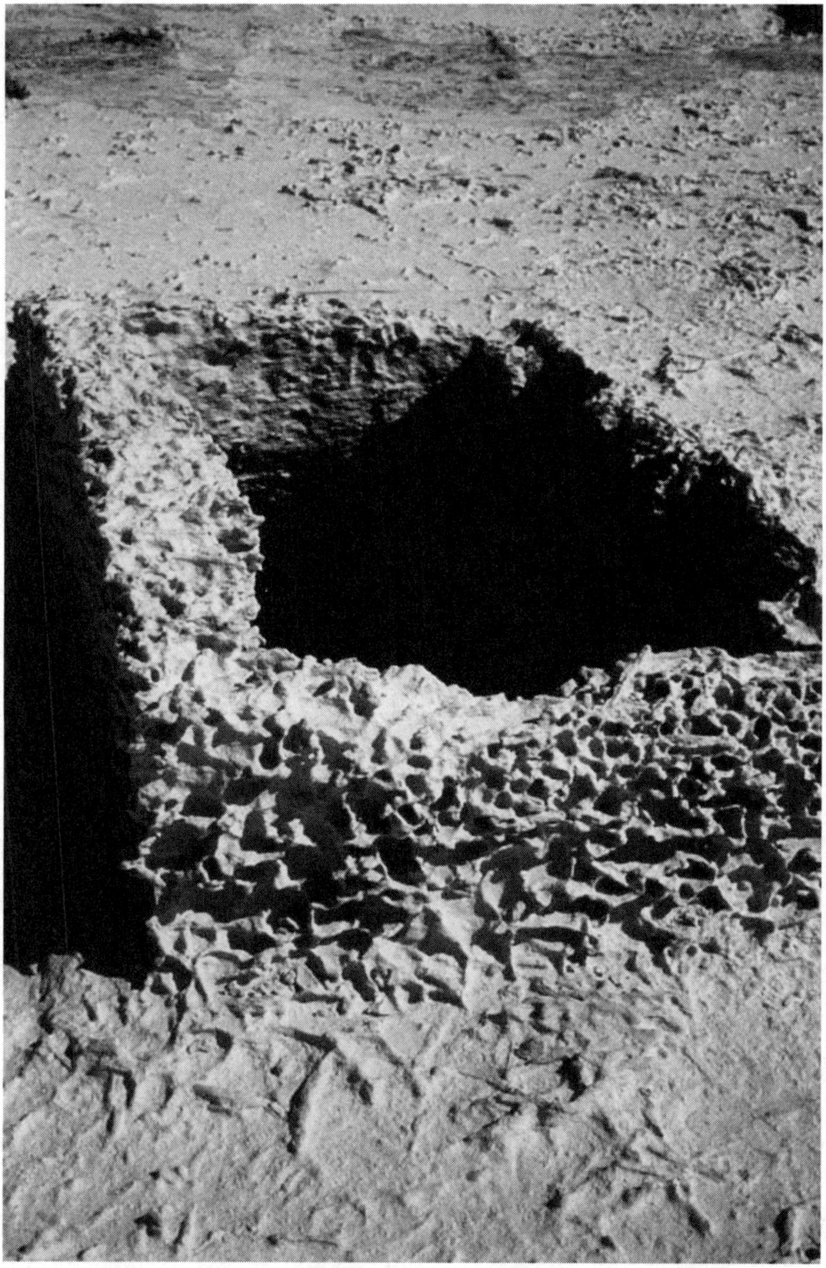

Fig. 60. Ras il-Wardija, the rectangular opening of a bell-shaped pit (photograph by the author 2001).

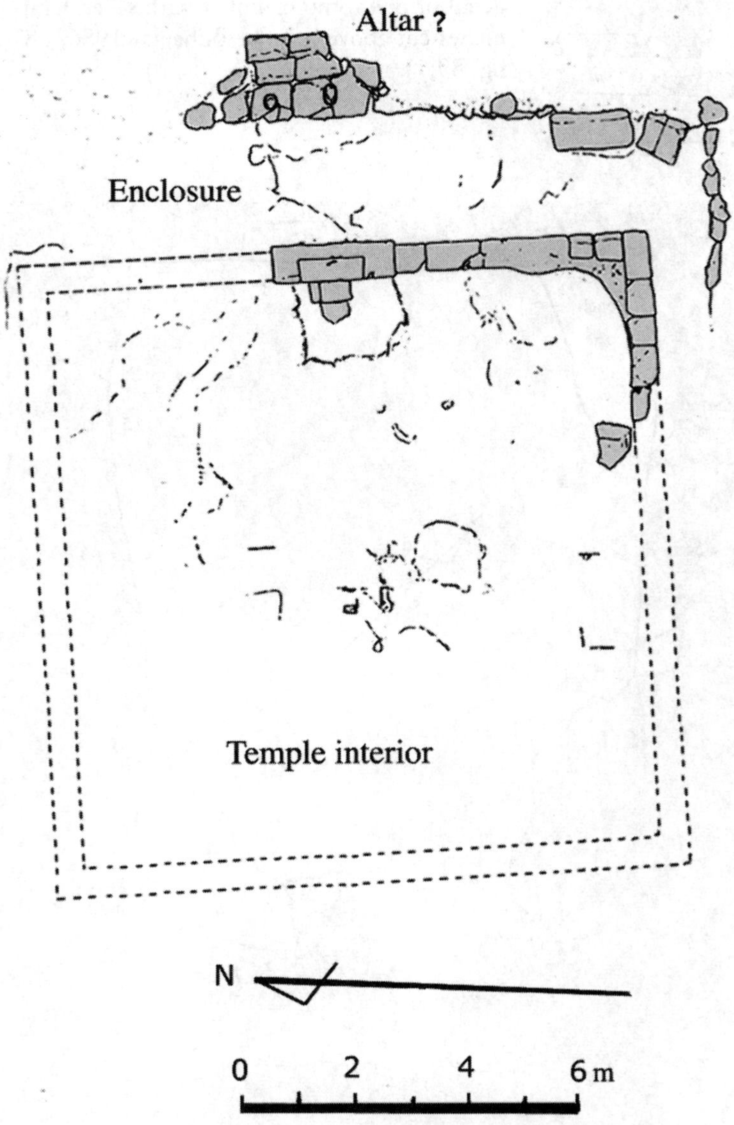

Fig. 61. Plan of the open-air temple at Ras il-Wardija.

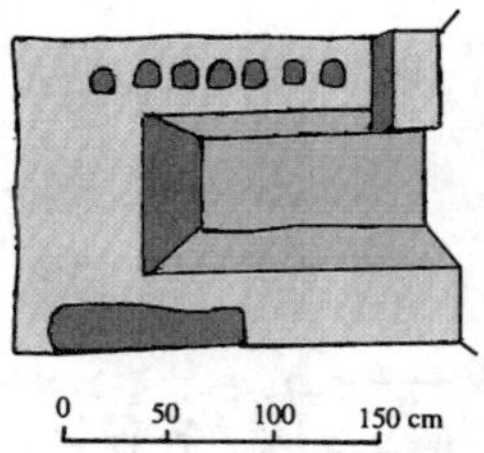

Fig. 62. Hypogeum 18, Binġemma (Mġarr), detail of one tomb chamber with seven lamp niches cut above it (after Buhagiar 1986, 287, fig. 89:1).

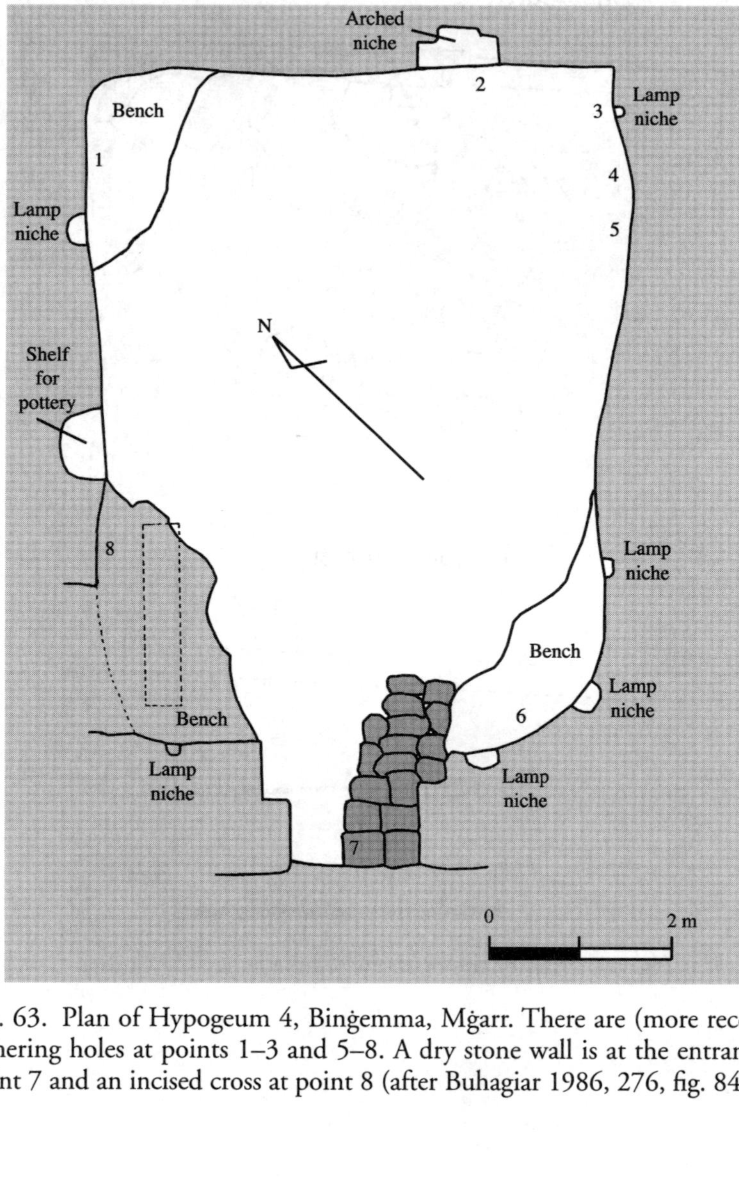

Fig. 63. Plan of Hypogeum 4, Binġemma, Mġarr. There are (more recent) tethering holes at points 1–3 and 5–8. A dry stone wall is at the entrance, point 7 and an incised cross at point 8 (after Buhagiar 1986, 276, fig. 84:B).

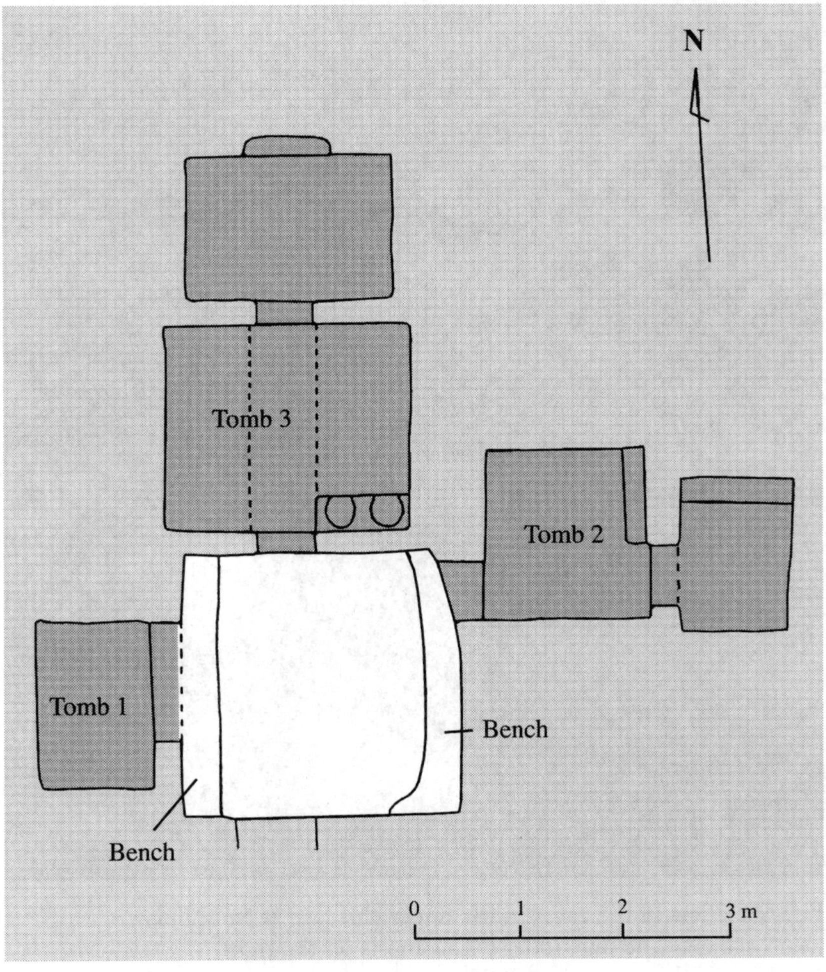

Fig. 64. Plan of Hypogeum 26, Binġemma, Mġarr (after Buhagiar 1986, 292, fig. 93:B).

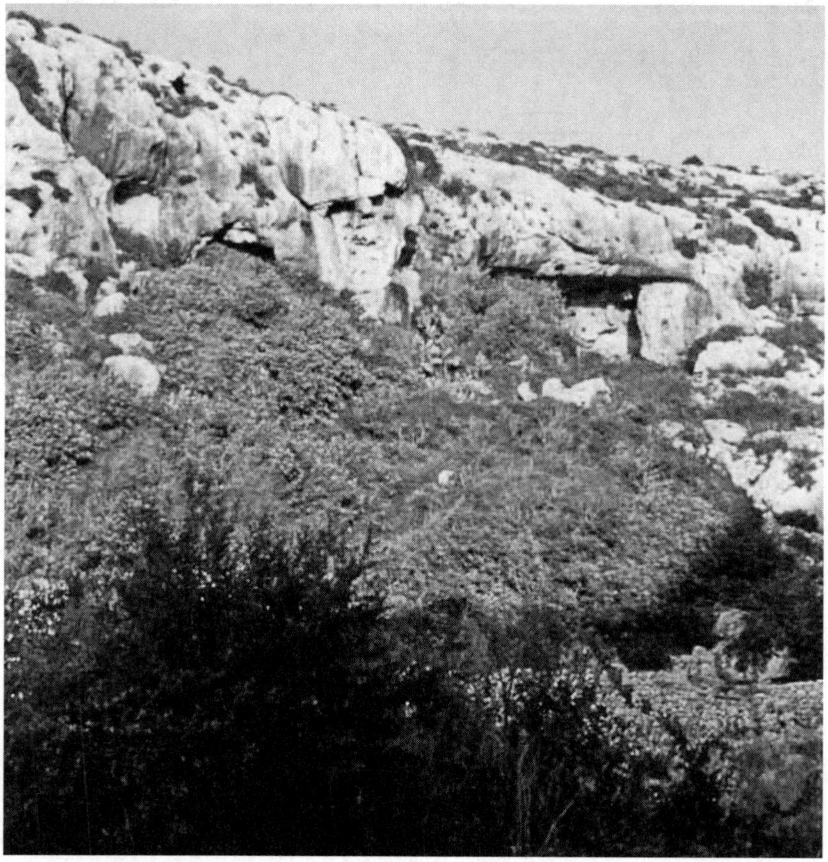

Fig. 65. View to the caves in the upper cliff face at San Niklaw, near Mellieħa; the one under discussion is on the right (photograph by the author 2003).

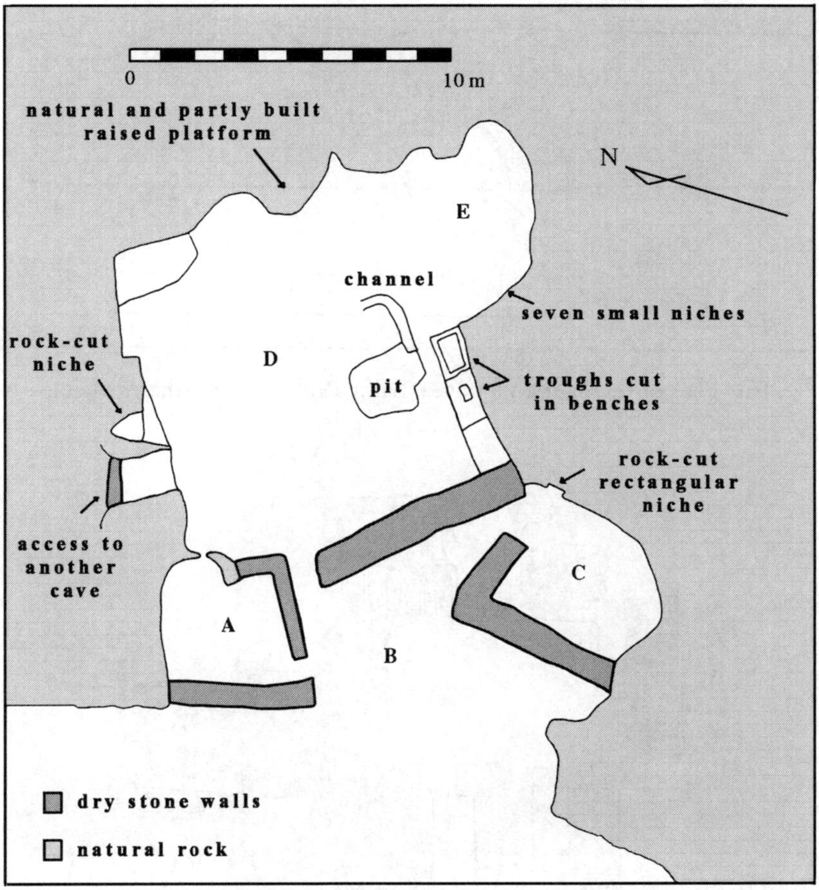

Fig. 66. Plan of the cave site at San Niklaw, near Mellieħa (after K. Buhagiar 1997, fig. 2).

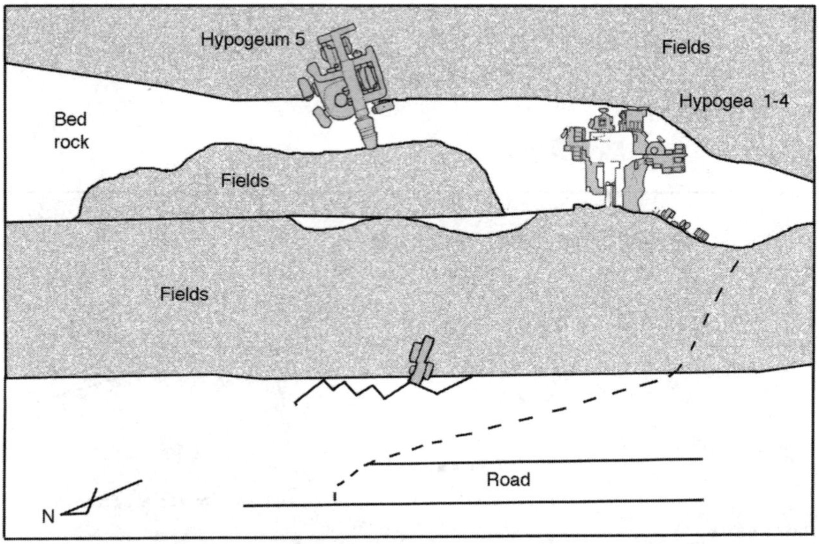

Fig. 67. Plan of the Salina Hypogea, Saint Paul's Bay, northern Malta.

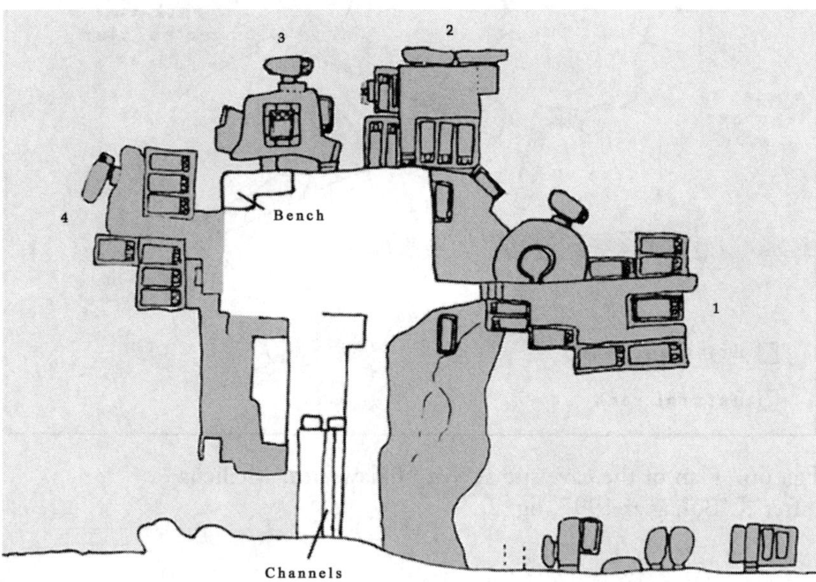

Fig. 68. Plan of Hypogeum 1 to 4 (shaded area) around the central rectangular open area (white area) that may have been a mithraeum (after Buhagiar 1986, 343, fig. 110:1 and Bonanno 2005, 332).

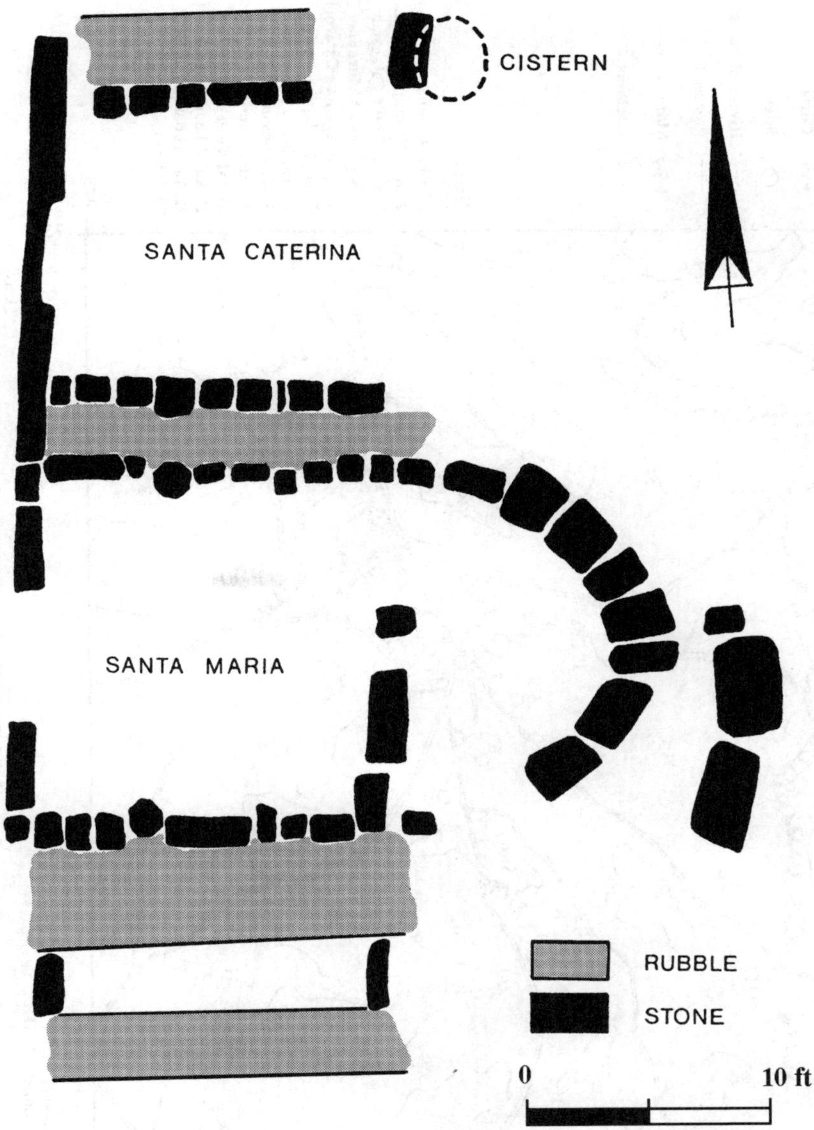

Fig. 69. Plan of the structures, Santa Caterina and Santa Maria, at Tal-Baqqari, near Żurrieq (after Murray 1923, vol. 1, pl. 5).

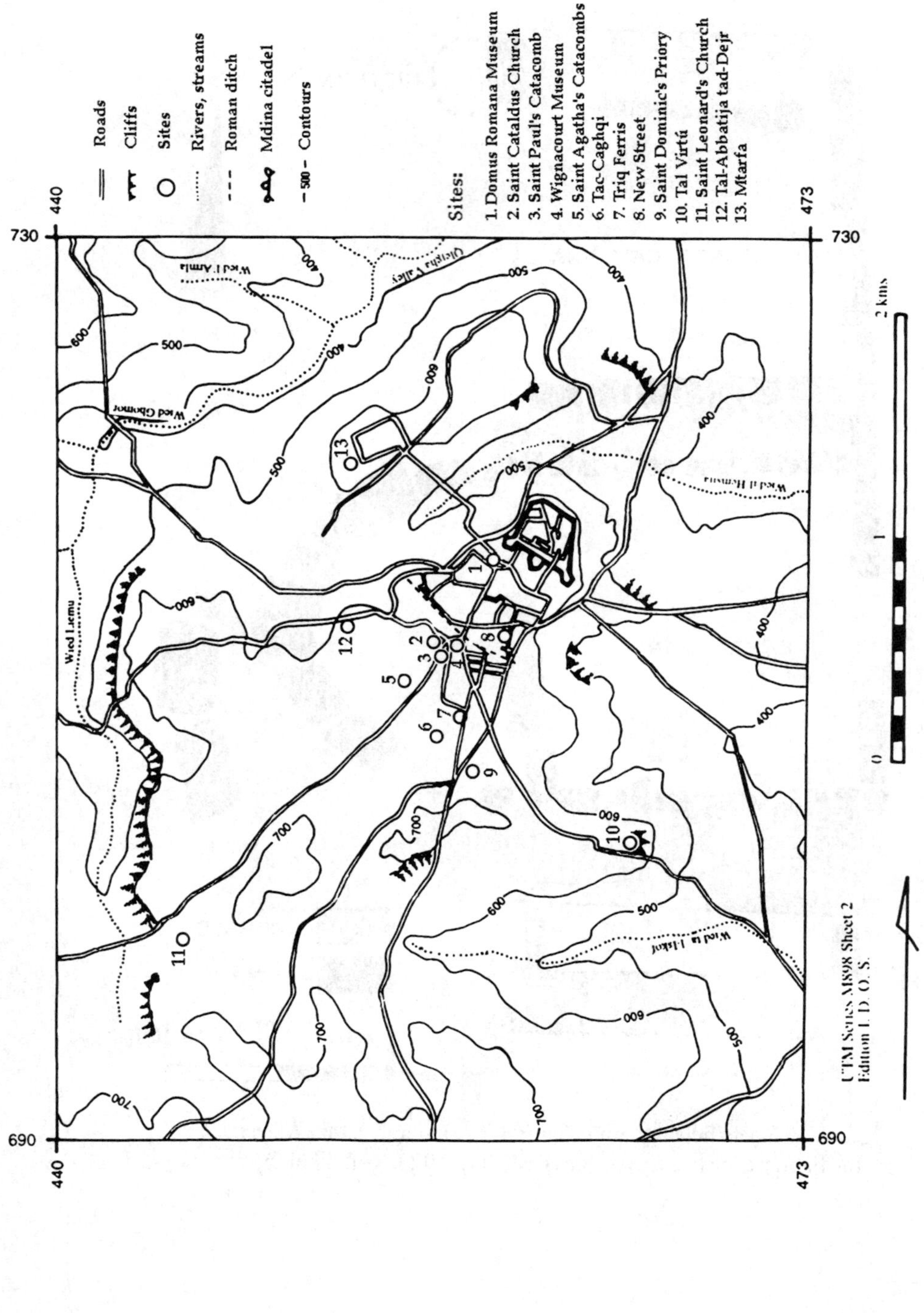

Fig. 70. Map of the Rabat area.

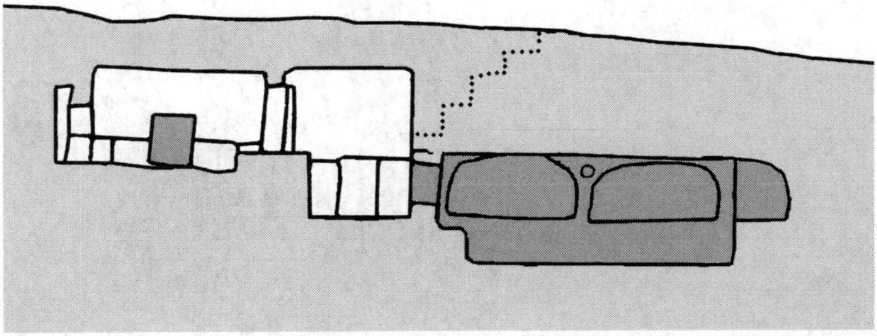

Fig. 71. Section of the 'Primary School' Hypogeum 1 (after Buhagiar 1986, 162, fig. 53:A). The possible mithraic chambers are in white, later tomb chambers and entrances are shaded.

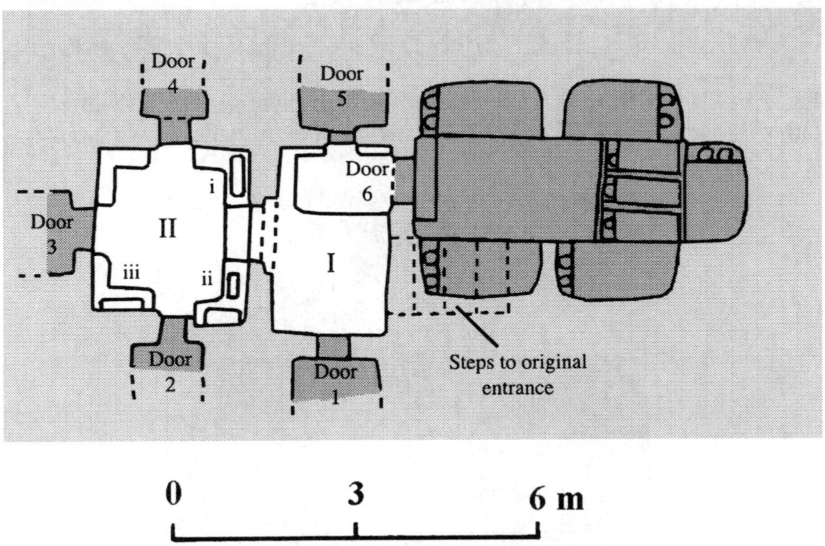

Fig. 72. Plan of 'Primary School' Hypogeum 1; the possible mithraic chambers are in white, later tomb chambers and entrances are shaded (after Buhagiar 1986, 162, fig. 53:A).

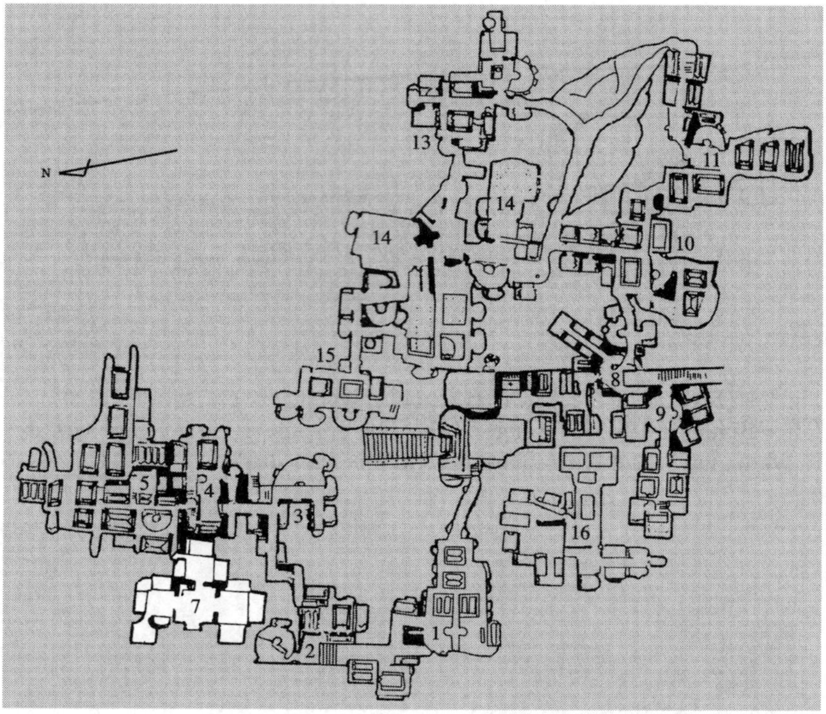

Fig. 73. Plan of Saint Agatha Catacombs with Hypogeum 7 in white (after Buhagiar 1986, 71, fig. 17:a, based on a plan made by V. Camilleri).

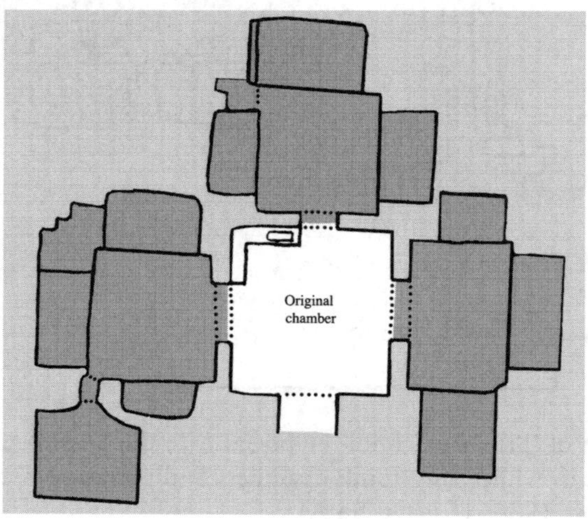

Fig. 74. Plan of Hypogeum 7, within Saint Agatha Catacombs (after Buhagiar 1986, 83, fig. 21:b). The possible mithraic chamber is in white, later tomb chambers are shaded.

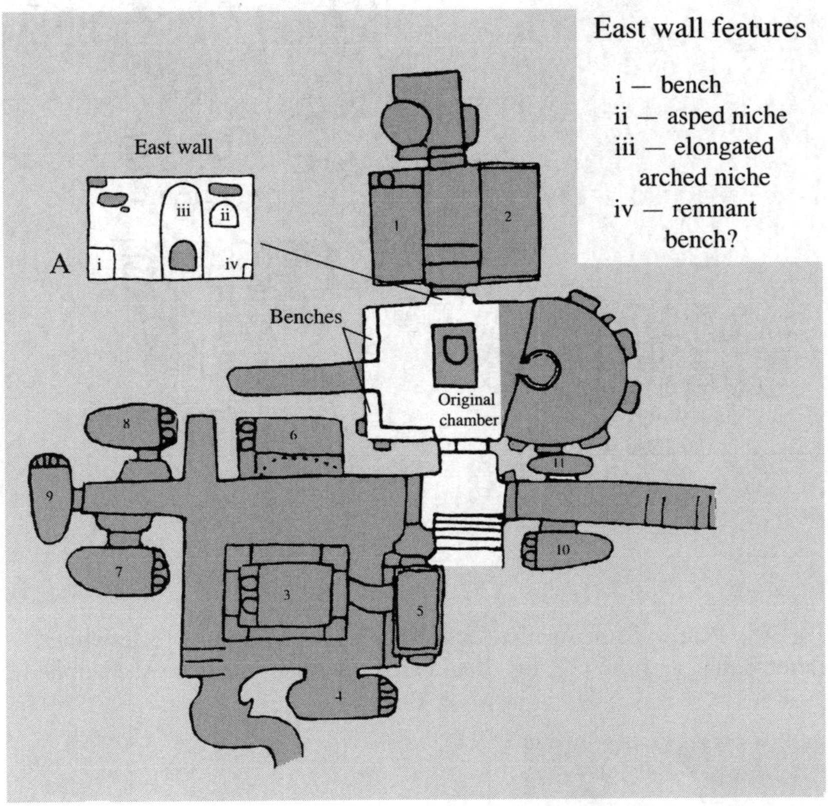

Fig. 75. Hypogeum 13, Saint Agatha Catacombs. **A**: View of the wall opposite the entrance with well-cut arched niche (cut through for an entrance possibly at a later date); (i) and (iv) are remnant rock-cut benches, (iii) may have been a niche for cultic figures, (ii) is a shelf. Other features (shaded) are probably later additions (after Buhagiar 1986, 87, fig. 23:1). **B**: The possible mithraic chamber is in white, later tomb chambers are shaded (after Buhagiar 1986, 87, fig. 23:a). The rectangle on the floor (shaded) is a door plug to one of the catacombs.

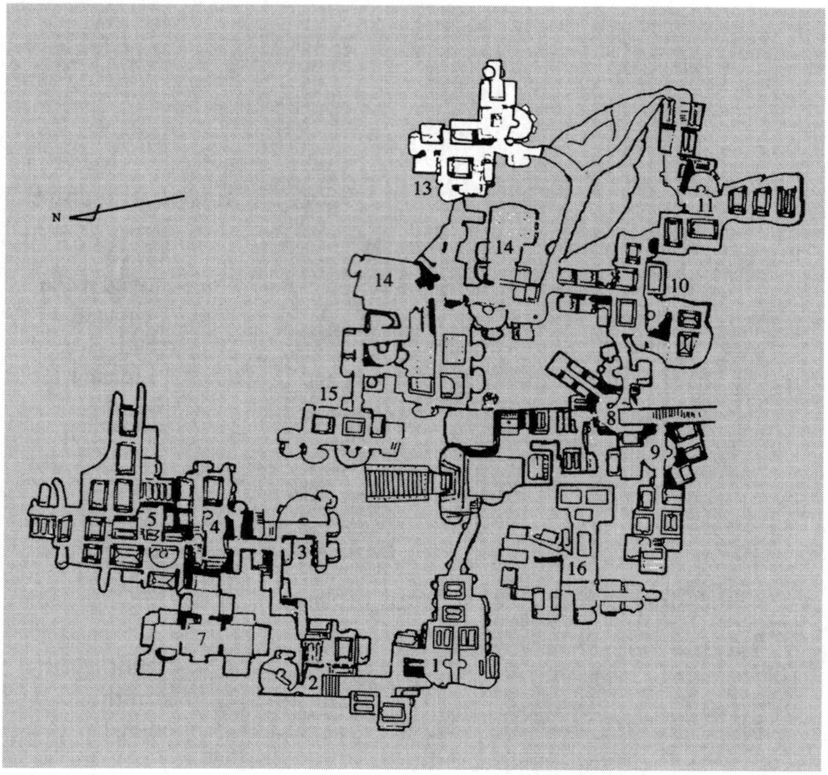

Fig. 76. Plan of Saint Agatha Catacombs with Hypogeum 13 in white (after Buhagiar 1986, 71, fig. 30:a, based on a plan made by V. Camilleri).

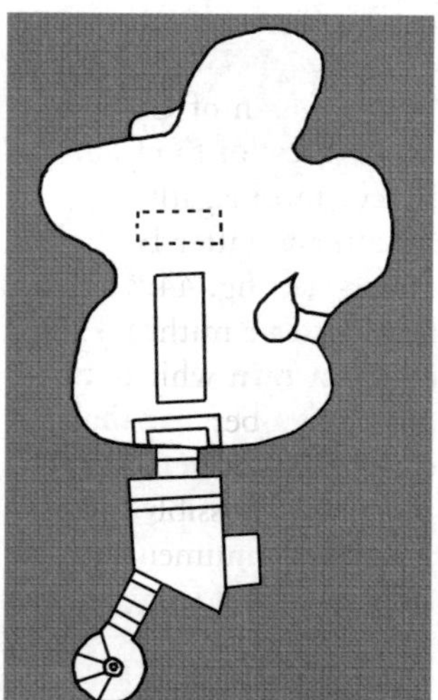

Fig. 77. Plan of Saint Maria della Virtú, Rabat (after Buhagiar 2007, 260, fig. 114:a).

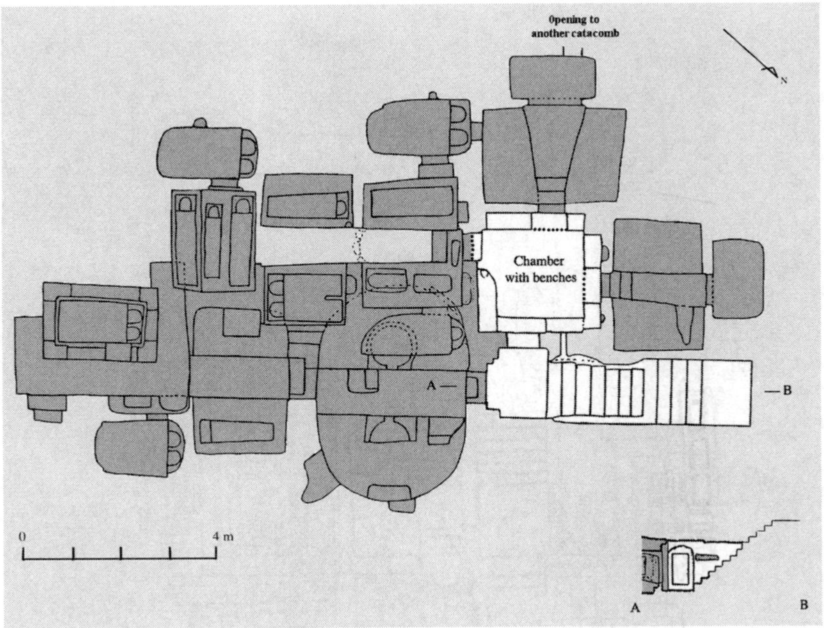

Fig. 78. Plan of Catacomb 6, in the cluster of Saint Paul – Saint Agatha Catacombs (after Buhagiar 1986, 103, fig. 27). The possible mithraic chamber is in white, later tomb chambers are shaded. Section A-B illustrates the well-made arched entrance to the chamber (after Buhagiar 1986, 104, fig. 28:A top).

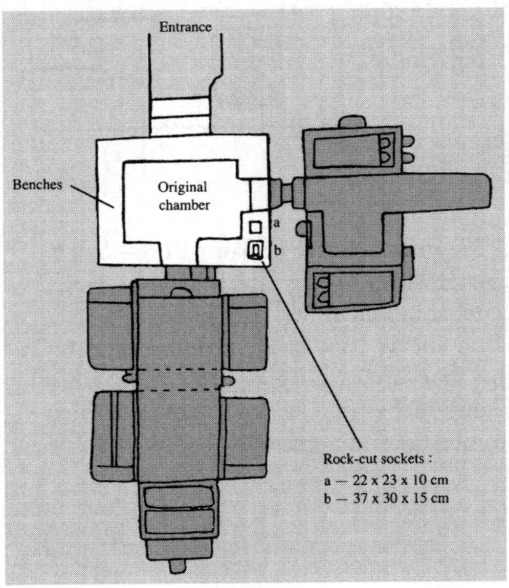

Fig. 79. Plan of Catacomb 20, in the cluster of Saint Paul – Saint Agatha Catacombs (after Buhagiar 1986, 136, fig. 44:B). The possible mithraic chamber is in white, later tomb chambers are shaded. Note rock-cut benches and socket possibly for a mithraic monument.

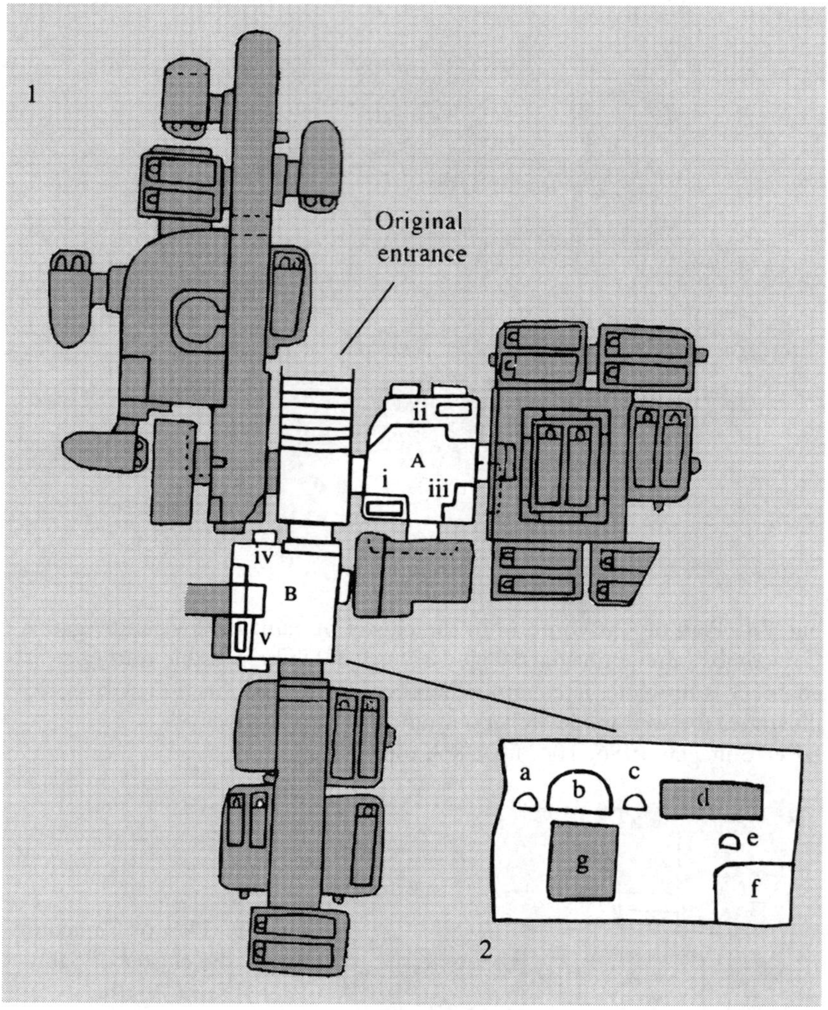

Fig. 80. **1**: Plan of Catacomb 22B, in the cluster of Saint Paul – Saint Agatha Catacombs (after Buhagiar 1986, 141, fig. 45:B). The possible mithraic chamber is in white, later tomb chambers are shaded; (i–v) are benches; later graves (i, ii and v) have been cut into the tops. **2**: The rear wall of the original chamber (after Buhagiar 1986, fig. 45:B, a) showing the arched niche (b), lamp niches (a, c, e) and remnant bench (f); a doorway to a gallery of tombs (g) and a grave (d) are likely to be later additions.

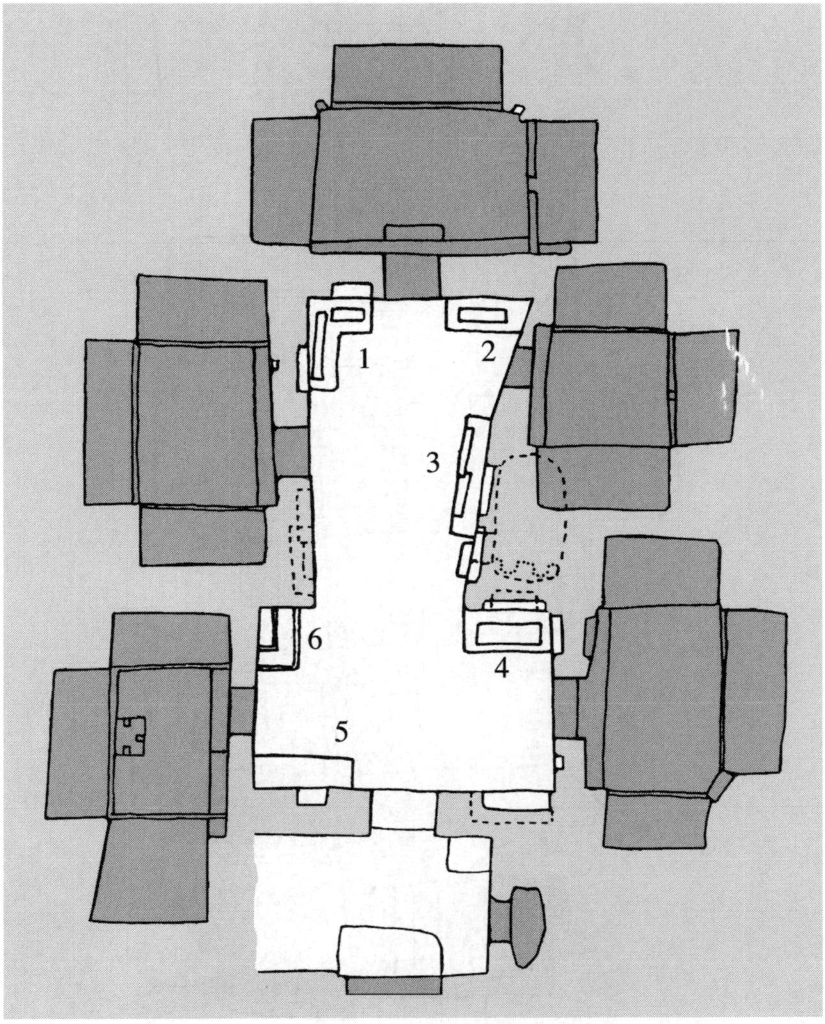

Fig. 81. The South-East Hypogeum, in the Secondary School Hypogea, Tac-Caghqi, Rabaṭ (Buhagiar 1986, 188, fig. 60:A). 1–6 are remnant benches, 6 may have been socketed to take a monument. The possible mithraic chamber is in white, later tomb chambers are shaded.

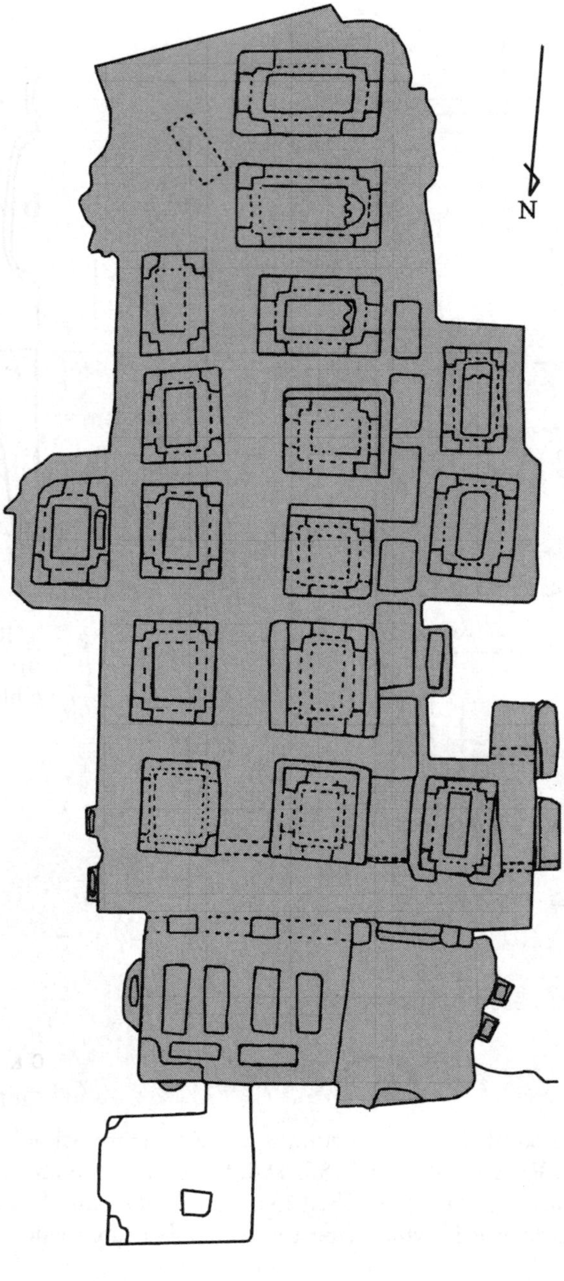

Fig. 82. Hypogeum 1, Abbatija tad-Dejr, Rabat
(after Buhagiar 1986, 203, fig. 65). The possible mithraic chamber is in white, later tomb chambers are shaded.

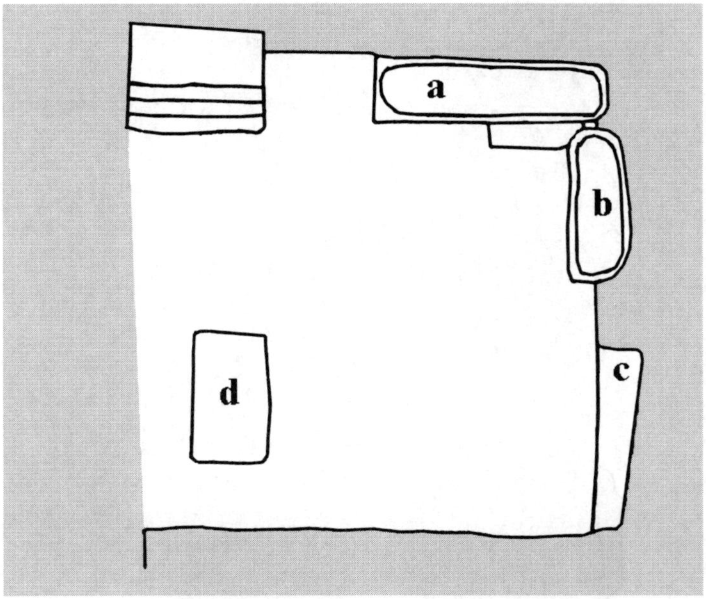

Fig. 83. 'The Rectangle', Abbatija tad-Dejr Hypogeum, Rabat (after Buhagiar 1986, 209, fig. 67:D); (a-b) are rock-cut benches with graves cut in the top; (c) niche; (d) stone block.

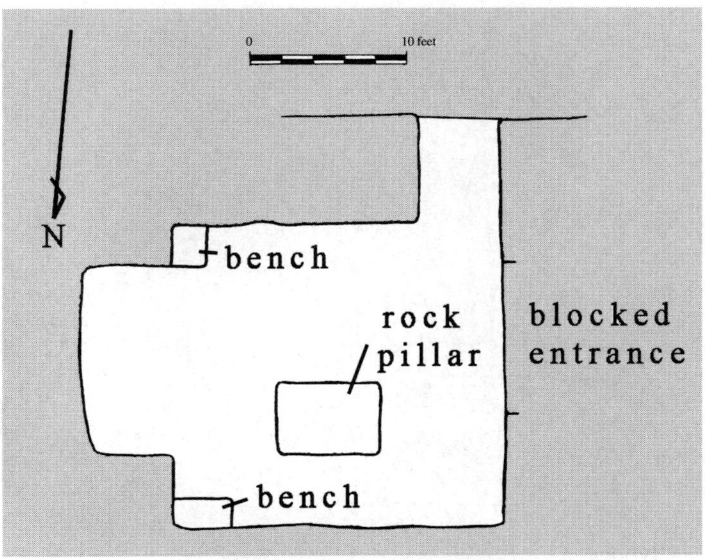

Fig. 84. 'The chapel', Abbatija tad-Dejr Hypogeum, Rabat, a possible mithraic chamber (after Buhagiar 1986, 209, fig. 67:B).

PRINTED ON PERMANENT PAPER • IMPRIME SUR PAPIER PERMANENT • GEDRUKT OP DUURZAAM PAPIER - ISO 9706

N.V. PEETERS S.A., WAROTSTRAAT 50, B-3020 HERENT